I MARRIED THE MINISTER

I Married the Minister

CYNTHIA PURSE

KINGSWAY PUBLICATIONS
EASTBOURNE

ISBN 0 86065 375 7

Cover design by Drummond Chapman

Printed in Great Britain for
KINGSWAY PUBLICATIONS LTD
Lottbridge Drove, Eastbourne, E. Sussex BN23 6NT by
Richard Clay (The Chaucer Press) Ltd, Bungay, Suffolk.
Typeset by Nuprint Services Ltd, Harpenden, Herts.

Contents

Foreword

I first met the Purse family five years ago, when my husband
Dave and I were invited to lunch at their home. Dave had
been on tour with Cliff Richard in Europe and had met
Eddie one evening in a Belgian hotel. I remember Dave
described Eddie as being 'a really good bloke—not at all
like a Baptist Minister!' On meeting him that day, I knew
exactly what he meant.

We were to discover that Cynthia was not what we
expected of a minister's wife either. They both have an
ability to communicate in a very fresh and 'unchurchy' way,
which is appreciated enormously by someone like myself,
who is unused to church customs and language. Like many
others, I have suffered at the hands of the media who have
shaped my image of a typical vicar and his wife. Cynthia
recognizes the problem in the early pages of the book. I
used to imagine a minister as a buck-toothed, balding and
out-of-date individual; while his wife was rather like a
clipper in full sail with the entire contents of her flower
border plonked on her head for church services and fête
openings!

To be fair, I have not yet met a couple like that, but
perhaps behind the caricature there lies some degree of
accurate observation? The interesting thing is that we seem

to view the clergy (along with politicians and celebrities) as fair game for criticism and cruel humour. Somehow we assume that when people enter into these professions, they relinquish their rights to being fallible human beings. People in the public eye simply should not make mistakes—or get hurt when ridiculed or criticized!

I remember quite clearly a comment made five minutes before going on air 'live' on *Blue Peter*. I was seven months pregnant at the time. A lady onlooker turned to me and said, 'How on earth you have the face to go on television looking like that I don't know. I mean, you're enormous, aren't you?' I got through the programme but went home shattered. That lady was not meaning to hurt. She simply saw me as the *Blue Peter* presenter, rather than a young wife expecting her first baby. I understood, but it did not stop the hurt. We do the same things to our church leaders, and they understand—but they still get hurt.

I believe that this book will be a tremendously practical encouragement to those men and women who are called to church leadership. However, I commend it more to those of us who fill the pews! Speaking as a pew filler (albeit a truly committed and involved Christian one!) I was embarrassed by some of Cynthia's comments. I recognized in myself how ready I have often been to condemn the man in charge. I know too how tempting it is to try to manipulate the leadership through their wives.

My husband Dave is the son of a minister and so knows first hand what kind of horrors the children of the clergy are often subjected to. Every relevant issue you can think of is given an airing, often with painful honesty! Cynthia remarks that 'of course it is absolutely essential that she [the minister's wife] possesses a vital, daily walk with God.' Undoubtedly she possesses such a walk as this herself.

I Married the Minister is not a book that will make you feel comfortable! If you are anything like me, you will put it down at the end of the last chapter and find yourself with a renewed commitment to pray for your leaders and their families, in order that it may be a joy for them to fulfil what the Lord has given them to do.

TINA HEATH
February 1986

I

Just Another Woman

I sat nervously on a chair in the front row. This was the bit I disliked most—waiting! I looked at my watch; still ten minutes to go. I shouldn't have arrived so early. Somewhere behind me two women were deep in conversation. I found myself eavesdropping:

'I wonder if she plays the piano?'

'Ought to. They sing a lot of hymns, you know.'

'Well, if not, I expect she'll do the church flowers. Mrs Wotsit's hopeless; she just dumps 'em in a vase. We need someone to do the flowers.'

'She'll have to take over the tea too, won't she? Jane and Elsie's always falling out over it. It needs proper organizing. Yes, she can do that.'

'Good job she's good with kids. They need three more teachers in the Sunday School, so she'll just have to help with that—and what's more, no one's been to visit me from this church these past six months, so I hope she'll get round and see us a bit more often than that.'

There was a slight pause. Then a hand rested on my shoulder, and the next remarks were directed to me:

'Hullo dear! Didn't see you sitting there. Have you come to speak to us today? We was just talking about our new minister and his missus. They've not come yet, but we've got it all worked out. They'll have plenty to do when they gets here. And what's more, we don't have to pay 'em very much, because she's doing some teaching in the school—ain't that good!'

I was speechless—and thankful that I wasn't the pastor's wife in this particular place! Having been married to a Baptist minister for over half my life, I have discovered that people's expectations of clergy wives vary quite considerably from place to place. Hopefully not too many are as demanding as my two friends at that women's meeting!

Some of us who are married to 'men of the cloth' are very conscious of what *others* expect from us, and this can cramp our being what the *Lord* wants us to be. The vicar's wife is, of course, just another woman with normal maternal instincts and feminine emotions. She will have her fair share of spiritual gifts, but no more than that, so that she will fit into the part of Christ's body where she and her husband have been placed. She may be a very warm, friendly, caring person; or she may be of a shy, sensitive nature. Whatever her personality, let her be herself. Don't expect her to lead the women's meeting if she is essentially a people-helper rather than a platform person.

When Abraham was called by God to leave his comfortable home in Ur of the Chaldees, and launch out into the unknown, we read that 'Sarah went too'. For her, his loving wife, it was a happy duty to follow her husband's divine call. Most clergy wives will not have been to Bible College to train for the job. Not many will have been 'called' to be a minister's wife, but assuming that as a couple they have always sought to know how they can best serve God together, the call is a joint one. They are 'one flesh', and she is his 'helpmeet', which does not mean that she has the academic, theological knowledge that her husband possesses, nor possibly the same spiritual wisdom. They complement each other, as with any Christian marriage—or are learning to do so—and her special gifts will not be the same as his, nor will his be hers. They are a team, and they are there not just to serve the local fellowship and community, but to be part of it, receiving as well as giving.

Such teamwork in our ministry, as well as in our marriage, is one of the lovely things about being married to a clergyman. Maybe some wives wouldn't want their men-folk under their feet for much of the day, but most of us in the Christian ministry count it a privilege to enjoy such togetherness in the work. And of course, when he is away for a whole day at a stretch, then we really can go to town with stripping a room, or missing lunch, or turning up the record-player to full volume—or whatever grabs us most!

One wintry morning my husband Eddie was breathing over the frosted windows of our car, when a young mum from round the corner passed him by. 'Good morning! Bit chilly, isn't it?' she said, and walked on. A few moments later she was back again: 'Excuse me,' she said, 'are you a vicar? Could you come and see me some time? I feel I need an anchor in life. Perhaps you could help me to find God!'

Wow! Just like that—the question we should like every-body to ask. I must add that it is very rarely as straight-forward as that, but nonetheless in these days of so much worldly unrest, when the man in the street feels powerless to stop the tide of political fervour and violence, many, many people are beginning to ask questions like these.

It was not long before Janet did find that Jesus could be the anchor she felt so much in need of. Her anxieties and insecurities did not melt away the moment she put her trust in him as her own personal Saviour, but she began to see them in a new light and found strength to cope with the 'fightings without and fears within'. I loved to visit her, to pray with her, to watch her faith grow as it was tested and tried. When her daughter was rushed into hospital for an emergency operation, she could actually see the Lord's hand in it all, and the experience helped to develop her trust in him.

Eddie and I were in it together. It is *our* ministry, not just his! I am sure that a plumber's wife could never become so involved with a customer's faulty ballcock valve or blocked drain as I can with my husband's concern over a hurting soul. There are many pressures, it's true, but this is one of the great joys.

Because they are a team together, a clergy wife's first duty must be towards her husband. She is there to enable him to exercise his calling as preacher, teacher and pastor of his congregation. He will spend a lot of time absorbing other people's problems and hurts, so much of her thought and energy will go into making a home where he can relax.

Life in a minister's home can be very taxing, often tiring. It becomes a counselling centre, a catering headquarters, a study, a meeting place, a hotel, an office, a clearing house for all sorts of problems, as well as a family home. To create a haven of rest in the midst of all this sometimes calls for great ingenuity on the part of the lady of the house, but make it she must endeavour to do. It is part of the 'cherishing' that we vowed on our wedding day. Unnecessary tensions at home have, on occasions, caused an ordained man to renounce his calling.

John was one of them. For six years he struggled to keep up his responsibilities within the church where he was minister. Ordained in middle life, he had stayed in the district where he and Margaret had spent the early part of their married life. She had continued the very active social life which she had led previously, and had also felt it necessary to take a part-time job, because when John entered the ministry they had suffered a severe drop in income. She also liked to be involved in a wide range of church activities, as this seemed the right thing for a minister's wife to do. John himself became more and more frustrated as his busy wife grew increasingly less interested in him or her home. Meals were hardly ever served on time, the housework was neglected to such a degree that he felt embarrassed to take anybody home, and tempers wore thin. He couldn't cope, and sadly dropped out of the ministry altogether.

And such tensions are not always caused by domestic circumstances. Sometimes it is because the minister's wife allows herself to be manipulated by members of the church congregation, and she fires their ammunition at her husband! I hate to say it, but usually it is the women of the church who will endeavour to use their vicar's wife to put forward their complaints, mostly over niggly, unimportant issues, but even these can be a source of great irritation in the manse or vicarage.

Perhaps the word 'loyalty' is important here. Her first loyalty is always to her husband, certainly in front of other people. If she disagrees with any particular stand he may take, let them talk it out together, but never let them openly take sides against each other. The enemy of souls is delighted when he sees division in the camp, and we are just playing into his hands if we let this sort of thing happen.

Part of the role of the clergy wife is to protect and encourage her husband in the face of opposition. He will be criticized, sometimes in her hearing. Some people will be constantly demanding his attention and even wasting his time. Mrs Vicar will frequently find herself in the middle of such things, and will have to wear the hat of a diplomat where the parishioners are concerned, and an encourager when with her husband.

Apart from providing a comfortable atmosphere at home—protecting him from the vultures—what else can we do to help our partners? Quite a number of purely practical things, I think. In the United States, it seems that most clergymen have a secretary, but here in England the pastor's wife is the one who usually fills that role. I know one longsuffering lady who every week types up all her husband's sermon notes. My husband has his own form of copyright—nobody else can read his writing, not even me—so fortunately I've been let off that particular task!

Another of my friends would, during the early days of their ministry together, sit patiently through a 'practice run' of her husband's Sunday sermon each week, and endeavour to offer helpful criticism!

That constructive criticism need not be concerned only with the content of the sermon. It might well be to do with some irritating habit which spoils his delivery.

'I can't look at the man when he's preaching,' one church member confided to another, as they left the morning service one Sunday. 'He scratched his nose sixty-seven times this morning!' (Which rather belied her words—her concentration must have been quite intense to have come up with such an accurate assessment!) 'I wish she'd tell him.'

Probably 'she' is the only person who could tell him. Certainly one would hope that any criticism 'she' might offer would be lovingly given, and therefore more readily received than if it came from a different source. He is *their* spiritual leader, teacher and pastor; he is *her* team-mate, lover and partner for life.

A well-known Christian preacher mounted the steps of his pulpit one Sunday morning. Sitting right at the back of the crowded church, in a corner seat, was his wife. A visitor slid in beside her, obviously surprised to see the church so full. Halfway through the service, while the offering was being taken, she nudged my friend in the ribs and asked in a stage whisper, 'Is this your regular man?' Mrs Vicar nodded and smiled. Then came another question, this time a little louder, 'How long have you had him?' 'Forty-two years,' answered my friend. 'My, he must be good,' came the astonished reply. Yes, he was her 'regular' man, in more ways than one, and she his most devoted parishioner.

One more thing I feel that we, as clergy wives, can do to support our men in their calling is to uplift their public image as far as we can. It seems that the dog-collar is often an object of derision. The flabby, meek and mild personage so often depicted in television drama as representing 'the church' is far removed from the true image of a man of God! Surely, to lead people into a closer relationship with their Maker, to teach them the deep things of God, to help them through the crises of their lives, to offer advice and wisdom on a multitude of personal problems, requires men of great integrity and strength of character. All this, as well as a large share of self-discipline, time and energy put into sermon preparation, and coping with the limelight of the pulpit for a few hours each week, is what a minister's life is largely made up of.

However, the image of a parson held by the majority of people in our land complies with that portrayed on television—for that is all they know. The sad part of it though is that this is also their view of Christianity—and probably of Jesus. There might not be an enormous opportunity for clergy wives to set the record straight, but in the places where we do have influence—at our children's school, in the local shops, at the hairdressers, or wherever we circulate—there are many openings for Christian witness, and also for projecting a true image of the ordained ministry.

If the wife's first responsibility is towards her husband, her second must be towards her family. It is great when our children grow up with a loving concern for others, having learnt this from parental example, but it's a tragedy when they have seen such a concern demonstrated only at their expense, and have developed a feeling of personal rejection because of it. This is perhaps one of the greatest dangers of bringing up a family in a home where other people's problems are a large part of daily living. We shall be discussing conflict which arises between church and family commitment in a later chapter, not just from the point of view of Christian ministers, but where it affects any Christian family.

So what about the role of the minister's wife within the church and its congregation? It will take varying forms, depending on her own special abilities and the needs of the local fellowship. Ideally it cannot be good to have more than one major responsibility, be it the women's work, a Sunday School class, leading the catering committee, heading up a team of church visitors—or whatever. If she were to take it all upon herself, others who are also very well equipped to do some of these things would be deprived of the privilege of serving their Lord. But nonetheless some churches are content to flog a willing horse. And, strange to say, such people also expect her to have a dazzling, dynamic personality, find plenty of time to pray for everyone by name, attend all the church meetings, never find any of it boring, never be too tired to carry out her duties—oh, and just like the Queen, she should smile and be happy at all times!

2

Life in a Goldfish Bowl

The winter of 1963 was a hard one. The day we moved into our first home, we first had to cut a path through thick snow. It had drifted halfway up the windows, and that little flat offered a very chilly welcome, but it was home!

For any young couple I suppose setting up home for the first time is an exhilarating, as well as sometimes traumatic, experience. For us it was a particular novelty, because it meant that our whole way of life was changing. He had been an estate agent, I a humble bank clerk—each of us clocking in from nine to five, more or less. Following that we had both been to college for a couple of years, and suddenly here we were, having to take quite a lot of responsibility, give support to the weak and advice to the perplexed, all with so little previous experience of such things.

Coming fresh from Bible College I think we felt we were fully trained and in possession of most of the answers. In some ways, life in our first pastoral charge was quite a rude awakening! We discovered that office hours were a thing of the past. Our working day would begin at a normal hour, but often did not end until gone bedtime. Evening meetings started late in that place, because it was on the edge of commuterland. City businessmen were not usually home

and fed and free to venture out until mid-evening. Sunday
School classes, youth fellowships, and such things that had
once been our spare-time activities, a refreshing change
from the daily grind in the office, were now our work.
They, and the responsibility of them, were now there, all
the time!

In those early days it was no easy task to adapt to the
pressures of this new way of life. Having been able to sit
almost anonymously in the pew of the large town church
from which we had come, the jump from pew to pulpit was
quite a big leap. Although I myself did not quite land in that
exalted position, as someone has described it 'six feet above
contradiction', I still found my own situation quite different
from all I had known before.

Suddenly my husband belonged to other people! They
kept him talking late into the night, he always seemed to be
rushing off to somebody in need. He was often preoccupied
with other people's troubles. I felt like crying out: 'Hey, did
you marry me—or your church congregation?'

Penny felt the same. She was married to Paul, a bright
young curate, tall and dark, with laughing eyes. He had a
way of making people feel that they mattered to him, and as
he matured in his ministry, this was to be a great asset. But
in the early days it spelt a great deal of emotional trauma
for some of the young girls in his parish—and also for his
shy, sensitive wife. Of course, the girls hung on his every
word, and made no effort to disguise the fact. Yes, they
really did want to know about following Jesus, but if they
could talk over their personal difficulties with Paul, that
made it twice as interesting.

Penny found this particularly difficult to handle, and
confided that there were many times in that first church
when she wished they could both have been 'just ordinary
people, living in a semi-detached, with boring jobs during
the week, who spent their weekends in the garden'.

I believe that for many of us, having a husband who to

some extent is a public figure, can be a hard thing to cope with. Often we would just love to melt into the background and be one of the crowd. But of course it does have its compensations.

Most people, Christians included, must find friends and make a new life for themselves when they move to a new area. I suppose one of the perks of being public property is that there is always a band of people ready to receive us and anxious to be friendly.

The day we moved into a new situation a few years ago was memorable. The removal men had packed our furniture the previous day, so that we could make an early start for the eighty-mile journey. On arrival in the town which was to be our home from now on, we collected the key to the manse from one of the church members, who invited us to pop in for lunch at midday. We then walked into the empty manse to find that it had been scrubbed and polished in every nook and cranny, ready to receive its new occupants. The garden had been tidied, and the grass scythed and mown. This was June, when everything grows apace, and the house had been empty since the winter! The crowning touch was a cupboard full of goodies in the sparkling kitchen!

By the time we went to bed that night we had flowers in the lounge and home-baked cakes and pies filling the larder shelves, and our two children had been personally invited to join the Sunday School outing on the following day. Only yesterday we had torn up our roots, after fourteen years in a loving Christian fellowship, but already we felt very much part of this new caring community. Their welcome was practical and gracious, and we appreciated it enormously.

However, despite all this friendliness on a fairly wide scale, a clergy wife often has to plod a lonely furrow. Because of her husband's position it is usually unwise for her to form a close friendship with another member of the local church congregation. If she does, jealousies and resentments frequently follow. Besides this we are there to pastor our people. They won't feel free to seek our help if there is a risk that their confidences will be shared with a bosom pal in a neighbouring pew!

Strangely enough, one of the places where a pastor's wife can feel most alone is in church! In twenty-three years of marriage I could count on my fingers the number of times that I have actually sat in church with my husband. I know that there are many Christian wives, some of whom may read this book, whose loved ones never ever accompany them to church, for one reason or another, and theirs is a very deep, constant pain. I don't belittle that at all, and know full well that my own personal feelings on this issue are minimal in comparison. However, to a shy and reserved minister's wife, it sometimes takes quite a bit of courage to walk into church week after week on her own. If she ever dares to show her reticence, she is labelled unfriendly!

One Sunday morning I sat myself down beside a lady who immediately slid a little further along the pew! I got to wondering, for a moment, if I had used the wrong soap that morning, so kept my distance—just in case. The gap between us remained right through the service, and at the end she turned to me and said, 'My dear, I am highly honoured to have you sit beside me.' I laughed—but she meant it! For much of her working life she had been 'in service' in a large house, and to her the minister and his family represented authority, in the presence of whom she had been conditioned to feel inferior!

Even people outside the immediate church circle sometimes hold us a little apart. I was registering for admission to a nearby hospital once, and the young lady filling in all my details asked: 'Do you work?'

'No,' said I, thinking that she meant 'are you a wage-earner?'

'Oh, what do you do with yourself all day?' she said.

'Well, my husband is a Baptist minister,' I replied, 'so...'
But before I could enlarge on that, she exclaimed:

'Oh, you do work,' crossed out 'housewife' and wrote in
'minister's wife'! I was most gratified that she recognized
that I was married to a man, and not a house, but I don't
suppose she would have altered the original entry had I
disclosed that my better half was a school teacher or an
engineer.

What is so special about being one of us? In God's sight,
nothing! 'You are all one in Christ Jesus' (Gal 3:28). 'For
God shows no partiality' (Rom 2:11).

We don't want to be different. We are not really any
different. But somehow people tend to put us in a separate
compartment. Their standards are high, and very often we
fail miserably to match up to those expectations. All this
can bring a lot of pressure to bear, especially in the early
days of ministry.

We live in a very odd world, where people in the public
eye are often exalted way above their station. Great
expectations are made of them, which they can in no way
fulfil. During recent years we have been privileged to meet
several who might be regarded as 'household names'. I
have been delighted to find that, despite the euphoria
which surrounds them, they are basically just ordinary
human beings like the rest of us. Their lifestyle may be a bit
different, but the same things make them laugh or hurt or
grieve. If their back itches, they must scratch it—they are
not superhuman in any way.

And neither is your vicar or his missus. Called to serve
God in that particular way, yes. Dedicated to bringing men
and women into a deepening relationship with Jesus, certainly. But still just an ordinary man and woman, with
normal feelings and emotions. Please don't put them on a
pedestal, and expect them never to make mistakes or have
any shortcomings.

There are lots of things we all do, sometimes unwittingly,

that hurt and upset others, things that cause misunderstandings, unnecessary faults. Often I echo the words of the General Confession: 'I have done those things which I ought not to have done, and have left undone those things which I ought to have done.' Donning a clerical collar, or merely being the one who launders it, does not make one exempt from these sins. In fact, with the responsibility of spiritual leadership there seems to come a great load of 'things which ought to be done', and so one is even more conscious than ever before of the sins of omission!

No, we don't always reach people's high expectations; often we feel lonely or 'put upon'. Let me tell you how this affected Anne. When she and her husband were first married, they threw themselves into activity within the local church, and much of their spare time was spent fellowshipping with other Christians and serving the Lord in the youth group. Everything they did was done together, and brought great happiness to them both. A few years and two babies later their level of involvement in church life became much greater. John gave in his notice at work, and accepted a call to the pastorate of a growing Christian fellowship in the Midlands, many miles from home. Anne, of course, was right behind him in this move. Before deciding to make the change they had prayed about it a great deal together, and shared their burden with many Christian friends.

The settling-in period in the new situation was an exciting time. John's induction service had seemed almost like another wedding day, with promises made, friends from distant parts joining to wish them well, and a sense of expectancy hanging over the future ministry within this company of Christian people. A few months later, when the novelty of the situation had worn off a little, the outlook seemed a bit different. Anne began to realize that some people were making very heavy demands on her husband, and to be honest she rather resented it. It seemed almost as though they could smell the dinner cooking, and deliberately chose that time to ring him up. Many times his half-eaten meal was pushed back into the oven, while he rushed out of the house in answer to an 'emergency' call.

Then there were the long evenings, coping alone with the baby's teething fever and tantrums. Much of John's pastoral visiting had to be done then, when his parishioners were home from work. On top of that, evening meetings took up two, or sometimes three, nights a week—often with protracted personal conversation afterwards. To Anne it appeared that she and John were drifting slowly apart. It had never occurred to her, on entering the ministry, that she would have to share her husband to this extent.

To some clergy wives this is perhaps the greatest problem which has to be come to terms with. In the course of his work, he will become deeply involved with a lot of people on a personal basis, some of them very demanding and possessive, most of them women! He can't always share their troubles with his wife. Much of what is discussed by other people with their vicar or minister is in strict confidence, and unless he chooses to tell her, it is not necessarily his wife's right to know about it. I wonder how many of us have a bit of Delilah in us, and would sometimes contrive to prise out of our nearest and dearest the deep secrets with which he may have been entrusted? While it must be good to 'share things for prayer', breaking confidences is another thing.

One day, a few years ago, I answered the door to a young lady bearing an enormous bouquet of flowers. The local florist's van stood outside. It wasn't my birthday or wedding anniversary, and I was convinced I had not yet died—but she assured me that this unexpected offering was definitely mine! Mystified, I slid the little card out of the envelope, and underneath the sender's name was the following: 'In deep appreciation of your willingness to lend me your husband for many hours recently'! Such tokens of thanks are rare, and I would neither expect nor desire people to register their feelings in this way—but that bouquet certainly brightened my day.

Philippa was another clergy wife who, like Anne, found that sharing her husband with other people was a most uncomfortable experience. When they arrived in their first parish she knew she would not see as much of Andrew as previously, particularly in the evenings. She adapted her day accordingly, so as to be with him when he was at home and not actually studying. The initial pastoral visiting they did together, which proved invaluable in getting to know the parishioners, and also making themselves known as a couple. Sometimes the vicar's wife becomes part of his 'baggage' in other people's eyes, rather than part of himself and his ministry.

She was also prepared to find herself and her husband constantly on call, and to open her home to all who needed them. Her big difficulty was accepting Andrew's pastoral ministry herself! Previously she had readily received spiritual counsel from her own pastor, but to seek such help from her own loved one she found acutely embarrassing. Because she was unable to communicate her feelings to her husband, he was quite unaware of her need, and yet it seemed to Philippa that he was totally preoccupied with other people's worries, at her expense!

It was just at a time when she was feeling particularly low, that an older lady in that church became increasingly concerned for Philippa's welfare, and proved to be the shoulder she needed to cry on. In a gentle, loving way she helped the young minister's wife to let go the emotional flood that had been building up, and paved the way for smoother lines of communication between husband and wife.

I believe that the minister's home is a very strategic target for the Enemy. His theory is to trip up the front runners of the pack, and the rest will collapse like a deck of cards. He is right, of course, all the time the congregation is blindly following close on the heels of their leader. Our brief though is to teach our little flock to look to Jesus for their example, and to learn how to stand on their own feet where their personal Christian faith is concerned. It is a very loving touch, and an act of grace, when a member of the fellowship can minister to the minister—or his wife. Sometimes Satan plays into the Lord's hand, by providing opportunities for such Christian grace to be activated. That elderly lady's ministry spread ointment on the hurt between Philippa and her dear one just when it was smarting most.

The sequel to this experience was equally far-reaching. Having come into the minister's home on a mission of mercy, this dear soul was made aware of another situation where she could offer herself. Since their arrival in the town six months previously, Philippa herself had never been to a mid-week meeting at the church, and in fact was not very often at the evening service on Sundays. Their children were not old enough to be left alone and, of course, she and Andrew could no longer take turns at going to these meetings, as they had done before. So our friend became a substitute 'Granny', and as such was gladly welcomed by the younger members of the manse household.

She was affectionately named Granaty (Gran number three). They looked forward to her fortnightly visits on Tuesday evenings, when she taught them to knit, crochet and embroider, and always finished with one of *Uncle Arthur's Bedtime Stories*, not nearly so sophisticated as *Dr Who* or *Star Trek*, but ten times as soothing and a far more fitting end to the day.

Twice a month she came to Sunday tea, and stayed on into the evening. In her younger days she had played the church organ, and now the music in her fingers flowed out again as, sitting at the piano, she taught her little charges all the favourite choruses remembered from her childhood. After the sing-song they played snakes and ladders, or ludo, and by popular demand this pattern remained unchanged for many months.

Philippa began to really feel part of the church fellowship now that she could worship there more frequently. And as for Granaty, she had found a very special joy in life again. Since her husband had died ten years previously, following a long illness, she had lived alone. Inwardly she still mourned for him, but the Lord Jesus was very precious to her, and she spent a lot of time praying for missionary friends and local needs. I suppose that it was through this ministry of prayer that she had first become aware of Philippa's inner needs, which in turn had led to her new status within the manse household.

Somehow I feel that there must be many more people in our church congregations who could exercise a valuable ministry of this kind in the homes of young Christian families. Babysitting is not listed in the New Testament catalogue of spiritual gifts, but it is a practical service which is highly prized by Christian parents, and often provides extra quality to the life of the babysitter. It is not just clergy families who would value a substitute gran. There are many couples in our churches today whose lives would be enriched if Mum and Dad could go together to the mid-week church fellowship meeting, or out to supper or a concert occasionally, knowing that their children were being cared for by someone with whom they felt totally at ease.

Throughout Andy and Philippa's stay in that town, Granaty was very much part of their family life, and maybe it is significant that, only a few weeks after they moved to their next pastoral charge, she went home to be with her Lord! I wonder if she ever knew what an important part she had played in helping one young clergy wife to adapt to life in the goldfish bowl?

3

Angels Unawares!

Gone are the days when Sunday tea at the vicarage consisted of thinly-cut cucumber sandwiches with the crusts removed, accompanied by china tea from a silver teapot, with the guests perching nervously on the edge of their chairs, making polite conversation! However, offering friendly hospitality is still very much part and parcel of life in a minister's home.

Over the years we have entertained some delightful people, ranging from rock stars to bishops, and many in between! Our visitors' book reveals many strange-sounding names, as often our guests have come from other parts of the world. Despite the vast divide in culture and custom, the bond of Christian love is something which continually surprises and delights me. Somehow we are all family; brothers and sisters in Christ. Our home is theirs during their short stay, and when they leave, it always seems as though a little bit of us has gone with them! At one time I used to worry about the catering when visitors were expected, but most of these people are used to travelling around, and seem able to cope with my cooking quite well.

Once I was floored. An African bishop arrived one Bank Holiday weekend, and as we sat down to supper he disclosed that he was a diabetic. On the menu that evening was a pasta-based meal, followed by meringues with raspberries and cream. The shops were closed for three days, and my store-cupboard revealed nothing more exciting within the permitted range of foods than four cracker biscuits and a few eggs. Had it not been for a neighbour's productive greenhouse, and the extras carried on the milkman's float next morning, our guest would have been in for a very lean weekend.

Another time we were expecting a team of five missionaries for an evening meal, prior to their conducting a special meeting in a town some miles away. It was midwinter, and icy cold outside. Just before they were due, all the lights in the house unexpectedly went out! The batteries in our only torch were almost defunct. A frantic rummage through various drawers produced only one small candle. Our guests arrived. They took turns to accompany the flickering candle upstairs to the bathroom. I served up their meal by the light of the gas jets on the cooker, and we sat down to eat. Just at that moment the candle spluttered and died. It was an interesting meal, quite hilarious at times. These angels I definitely entertained unawares—I don't even know what they looked like!

Giving hospitality on behalf of the local church is, on the whole, a happy exercise. Apart from entertaining travellers from afar, what better way is there of getting to know one's parishioners, or to help them share their burdens and worries, than over a meal, or even a cup of tea?

Jean and Glenn were a young couple whose spiritual life began when a Christian invited them home for a cup of coffee. They started to attend church after their baby died in a tragic cot death. It had been a traumatic period following the funeral, when both of them passed through weeks of alternate numbness and bitterness. One of Glenn's workmates had tried hard to tell him of the love of Jesus, but Glenn didn't want to know. How could there be a God of love who allowed such unnecessary tragedy?

It was a couple of months later when, one Sunday, Jean tentatively suggested that they go to church that evening. She couldn't really explain why she wanted to go, but just felt a kind of urge within her to do so. Although it was far from Glenn's mind, he was anxious to do anything that might help his young wife to find happiness, and so they went to church together on that sunny evening in May.

Looking back now, they find it hard to remember what they actually expected of that first visit, but certainly they were very surprised to find such a relaxed, friendly atmosphere, and could see instantly that the majority of people in that church had a quality of life which Glenn could only describe as purposeful and peaceful. They didn't recognize anyone in the congregation, yet almost everyone seemed happy to acknowledge them. Before they left the church, they had been invited out for coffee three times, and although they declined each invitation, they went home feeling somehow uplifted and accepted, and determined to go again the following week.

This time there were many smiles of recognition, and it felt like 'coming home' to be with friends. They gladly accepted the first invitation to après-service coffee, and really enjoyed meeting the Christian family who were their hosts. They had been there an hour or more, when a baby started crying in an upstairs room. Jean's heart missed a beat, but she found to her amazement that after the initial inner stab, she was able to cope.

It was no great surprise when, a few weeks later, both she and Glenn together committed their lives to the Lord Jesus Christ. The attitude of the Christians in that church, opening their homes and their hearts to a young couple in need, contributed greatly to their spiritual conversion. Our homes, whether or not we are 'in the ministry', are a useful tool for evangelism, and extension of Christian fellowship. Sometimes I wonder why we don't use them more!

Over the last decade or two some of us have been discovering the benefit of using them as neutral ground where friends and neighbours will come into a coffee morning or buffet lunch, with an evangelistic emphasis.

Wanda is a photographic model. She became a Christian five years ago, and was immediately anxious to tell the world of all that she had found in the Lord Jesus. Obviously in the course of her work she had plenty of contact with people who did not know the Lord, and she has helped a number with her testimony. Then she was invited to speak at a coffee morning about her experience of the Lord's goodness. A dozen women had met together in a Christian home, half of whom were visitors to the group, and had been attracted by the fact that they were to meet a real model. This was another world to them, and held an air of glamour and excitement. Wanda spoke a little about her work experience, lest her audience feel a tiny bit cheated, but the main emphasis of her talk was on how Jesus had transformed her life, giving her purpose and joy where there had been hurt and bitterness.

That was just the beginning. Since then there have been many such occasions, when Christian women have caught the vision of opening their homes for evangelism in this way. Friends and neighbours have come to know the Lord Jesus for themselves, and many have been helped to a deeper walk with him through Wanda's ministry.

A friend of mine, who is a widow, was also asked to share her experience of the Lord's strength through bereavement at a buffet lunch home meeting. Immediately she was on the same wavelength as many of the hurting lives there— those who were also suffering grief, but without personal knowledge of the peace and support to be found in Christ.

With a little imagination, I am sure that more of us could arrange such occasions in our homes, not perhaps with a photographic model, but with men and women from many different walks of life who have a vital Christian experience to share. Requirements: a few friends, a coffee pot, some thoughtfully-worded invitation cards, and a desire to spread the gospel. It is surprising how many people, who shy off at the suggestion of going into a church building, will happily accept an invitation into a Christian home.

Let me say something more about Jean and Glenn. Shortly after their arrival at the local church, they became aware that small house groups were meeting on a regular basis within the church fellowship, and soon found themselves assigned to one such group near their own home. Twice a month, on a Tuesday evening, they would meet together with a group of about eight or ten others from the church, sitting comfortably in their friends' lounge. The time would be spent sharing concerns for prayer and engaging in a discussional Bible study together. Others from the same church fellowship would be meeting at the same time in different parts of the neighbourhood, all studying the same Bible passage.

Jean and Glenn quickly made friends with the people in their group. There was Tom, a young man whose parents found his Christian experience very puzzling. At one time he had been quite a tearaway, but since his conversion a year previously his behaviour at home had been more considerate, and his friends and interests seemed to have changed a great deal. Tom longed for his mum and dad and sisters to know Jesus for themselves, and this was constantly the burden of his prayers. He found the house group a very strong support in his yearning for his parents, and as he worked through various crises in his working life.

Jane and Mary were sisters, one a secretary, the other a bank clerk. Neither of them was particularly vocal, but both carried an air of calm confidence in God, and they made a valuable contribution to the group.

David was an older man, with many years of experience in life as a Christian. Jean and Glenn really looked on him and his wife as their spiritual parents. They never treated Glenn's questions or Jean's uncertainties as trivial. Indeed, the house-group situation was one where they both felt perfectly accepted, perhaps partly because of its intimate size. It was a tremendous help to them both in their early Christian life. In a few months' time they would all disperse into different groups, and get to know other members of their church fellowship at this deeper level. Everyone who had opened his home for such a group had found it a special joy to serve the Lord like this, and, somehow, the people who came appreciated the informal surroundings and being able to share ideas and thoughts together.

Once, when I asked someone if we could hold a Young Wives' group meeting in her home, her reaction was to recoil in embarrassment: 'But my home's not good enough, and I can't make cakes like Jenny or Mary....' I have been to her house lots of times. It is a warm, welcoming, comfortable home. The carpet may be a little threadbare and the settee has a darned patch, but somehow the happy, cheerful atmosphere of the place overrides all that. As for the cakes, it is a pity that Jenny and Mary are such good cooks! Perhaps the rule of thumb for refreshments following meetings held in the home should be just tea and biscuits. Then nobody would feel unable to provide adequate hospitality.

Of course there are a multitude of meetings which it is deemed wise to be held in the minister's home. A vicar I know has a meeting going on every night of the week in his dining room, though that does seem a little extreme! Our own manse has been used for a variety of events, and each has made a special contribution to the life of our home.

At one time we lived in a cul-de-sac, and our neighbours were most intrigued by the throng of youngsters who flocked down the road into our house on Sunday evenings. 'Don't they spoil the furniture?' one curious woman asked me once. I must admit that until that moment the thought had not occurred to me. Actually they mostly sat on the floor anyway—too many to use the chairs. Later on, the church members, also conscious of the fact that perhaps they had 'spoiled the furniture', kindly gave us a brand new lounge suite!

It is difficult to be too house-proud in a home where people are constantly coming in and out. Following a girls' Bible class in my living room recently, one of them was collecting up some quiz questions which had been stuck in strategic positions around the room during the meeting. She ran her finger over the top of the mirror: 'Cynthia!' she exclaimed, holding up a furry, grey finger. 'You haven't done your work!' As the blush began to rise on my cheeks, another girl flew to my defence: 'Well, she can't do the one hundred and one other things she has to in the church, and all the dusting too, you know!' I was most gratified, especially when, the following week, the little horror who had found me out arrived, complete with headscarf, pinny and feather-duster, prepared to 'do the work I hadn't got time to do'!

Every now and then something happens which truly warms my heart. On Monday mornings we hold a prayer meeting in our church fellowship, which moves from house to house. One week, a short while ago, it was billed to be held in my home. I was feeling unusually tired. The room was a tip, following a very hectic weekend, and, dare I say it, I didn't even feel like praying!

As the ladies trickled in, I doubt if many knew how much I wished they hadn't come.

'How lovely to see you; you will have coffee?' Oh, what a hypocrite! The plastic smile of welcome faded each time I tripped to the kitchen to fetch more coffee, only to reappear as the tray was borne swiftly to refresh my guests.

Then Sylvia arrived, a lovely, gentle, caring person, a mother of five and a real pleasure to know. From behind her back she produced a sweet-smelling bunch of chrysan-themums: 'I thought our minister's wife would like these,' she said. 'You do such a lot for us.' They came with a hug

and a kiss too! It made my day. Gone was the excess weariness, the false front. I guess we all like to be appreciated,
and Sylvia's gesture of love that morning was so timely.

I must admit that I'm not always really eager to use my
home for meetings. Sometimes the room is spick and span
all day, and then, just before the people are expected to
arrive, the children decide to make a camp in it, or set up
the model railway, or drop an ice-lolly on the carpet. Often
it is a hassle to get everything ready to receive visitors, but
always we benefit from having fellowshipped with the Lord's
people under our own roof.

One year we returned from a camping holiday, exhausted
by various illnesses which had beset the family while away,
only to find that the Young People's Fellowship had booked
a meeting in our home on the following evening! Underneath, I suppose, we felt this was a little thoughtless on
their part, but imagine our surprise when during the meeting
they produced a cheque for a sizeable sum, which represented a 'whip-round' among themselves to enable us to
have a 'real' holiday a little later in the year! Almost
speechless with amazement, we mumbled our thanks for
such a totally unexpected gift, and added that we were
pleased they had earmarked it for a holiday, because if we
had saved that much money, it would have gone towards
something sensible like a vacuum cleaner. We probably
would not have felt justified in spending it on a good time.

Such was our even greater astonishment when, two days
later, a brand new Hoover Junior stood on our doorstep,
with a label attached: 'From two of your young people,
with our love.' From that day, ten years ago, to this, we still
don't know which two youngsters it was that had been so
generous and thoughtful.

Before that particular week had ended, we had also
received two lettuces, some runner beans, and a bottle of
sherry! The latter had been one of two bottles of very
high-class vintage, given to a young woman as a birthday

present. She had, together with her husband, very recently come to know Jesus as her Saviour, and this was her way of sharing her bounty with us.

Angels unawares? Yes, we have entertained many! I believe that the gift of hospitality is one which more Christians could exercise. One doesn't have to possess an Ideal Home to do it. In fact, most people feel much more comfortable when they are not likely to crush a cushion, or upset the coffee table display if they pick up a magazine.

One day a blind man was brought into our home. As he crossed the threshold his face lit up, and with great satisfaction he said, 'I'm all right here. It smells friendly!' I trust that Christian homes will always 'smell friendly', holding out a welcome to any who just drop in. Whenever hurting souls have been ministered to, or people have been born again under your roof, the lounge or kitchen becomes hallowed ground! More than once I have sat on my kitchen floor with a friend, while we have shared a burden together and prayed it through.

Once it was said of a certain house in Capernaum where Jesus was visiting: 'The news spread that [Jesus] was at home' (Mk 2:1, Good News Bible). If Jesus feels at home in our homes, surely other people will too! We shall have the great joy of sharing his love with all who come in—we might even entertain a few angels unawares.

4

This House Is Our Home

'But, Mrs Jones, we have always held the vicarage garden party in the vicarage garden! Where else could it possibly be held? No, it definitely can't be moved this year.' That being her final word, the telephone receiver was placed firmly onto its cradle.

Rosemary Jones, vicar's wife, recently arrived in this little corner of old England, was feeling more than a little put upon. Gardening was her hobby. The rambling vicarage left quite a lot to be desired for comfortable living, but the garden was like one she had always dreamed of. She had plans, big plans for its improvement. To be perfectly honest, she was more concerned about the garden than she was about the parish, and this was never so evident as on the day when Mrs Garden-Party Organizer rang to confirm the date in the church diary.

Rosemary did not want all and sundry trampling over her newly-sown grass, or sidestalls erected where she had plans for a rockery. The previous tenants of the vicarage had kept the garden very tidy, but it was so basic, so ordinary, so boring! To them it probably would not have mattered if a coconut-shy ball had bounced off the apple tree, but what if it landed on her tender camellia, or fell in the cold-frame?

After years of living in borrowed houses with rotten

'cabbage patches' she had at last landed one with a decent bit of ground, something that could really bring out the Capability Brown in her. But they wouldn't let her do it. This miserable garden party would ruin all her plans for this year's development. The more she fretted, the more she knew that eventually she would have to climb down 'for the good of the parish'.

It was with very bad grace that Rosemary finally gave way and, as it happened, it rained on the day, and so the event was held in the village hall after all! She laughs about it now. She learnt quite a bit about the things that really matter, distinguishing between the important and the more important, about give and take. 'It was a valuable experience,' she told me. 'I've still got lots of faults, but I think I know now where my priorities lie.'

Some have talked of moving house (and garden) in clergy circles as being the 'luck of the draw'. I suppose, to some degree, it is a bit like that. Clergy houses vary considerably in character and suitability for their purpose.

When I was very young, I remember visiting a vicarage that seemed to be little more than a passageway between the church building and the outside world. Almost everyone who attended any meeting at all in the church, be it on a weeknight or on a Sunday, seemed to spend some time in transit, either in the vicarage kitchen, or the lounge, or the spacious hallway. On Sunday mornings, during the worship service, you could even smell the midday lunch cooking, and it was said that some of the parishioners could tell you what the vicar had for lunch three weeks ago—they kept a weekly record! My friends who lived there didn't seem to mind their lives being so very public, but others I know find this sort of thing very difficult to come to terms with.

When Jane moved into vicarage number three it was not this kind of crowded, public home-life that bothered her. The house itself was a great barn of a place, built over a hundred years ago, and a residence of character in its own way, but she wilted at the thought of furnishing, cleaning and heating it. Their previous home had been a comfortable, four-bedroomed, modern, detached house with a small garden which was well-stocked and sensibly landscaped. Now she and her husband had half an acre to tend, as well as the Victorian mansion.

'How on earth they expect us to cope with the parish as well, I've no idea,' she cried. The ceilings and windows were high, the rooms themselves were enormous, and it was a route march from dining room or lounge to kitchen, even to pop the kettle on for a cuppa!

Three years and one brand new vicarage later, her initial horror had almost turned into affection for the dear old house. But impractical it certainly was in the twentieth century, and the old had to make way for the new. The new house was erected on the half acre of ground, had all mod. cons. and was very pleasant indeed, but somewhere in Jane's heart there lurked a touch of grief over the loss of 'the old place'.

Making a home out of a house frequently exercises the ingenuity of a clergy wife. During her married life she will live in many different places. Rarely will she have had a say in the choice of their residence. Sometimes the previous occupants' taste in decorations and embellishments will offend. Carpets and curtains can be a nightmare. Frequently left behind by their predecessors, often incompatible with the newcomers' furniture, they are usually tolerated for the first three or four years; then one wonders if it is worth changing them, as there might well be a move on the cards in the forseeable future!

Sometimes, of course, the change-over of houses is a definite improvement. At the beginning of Lent one year, I went along to an inter-church home-study group, which was held at a vicarage in the next parish. It was reputed to be the most beautifully placed church-house in all Sussex, and I was glad of the opportunity to spy it out! Having crunched up the tree-lined drive, I was admitted into a beautiful oak-panelled hall and then ushered into the lounge. A fire blazed in the inglenook fireplace, and the room felt warm and welcoming. From the patio windows I gazed on acres of winter-swept fields stretching to the gently rolling downs in the distance, and just outside, would you believe, there strutted a pair of peacocks! The latter belonged to a nearby country park, but apparently spent much of their time adorning the vicarage lawn. Certainly this lovely home deserved its reputation.

In the affluent village where it was situated, it was quite acceptable for the parson to live in comparative luxury. It would have been a different story, of course, in the centre of a large city. Perhaps one of the qualities required of a clergy couple is that they be adaptable to different cultures, happy to identify with the parishioners, whatever their situation. This has to stretch to our living quarters, as well as our place in the local community.

Nonetheless, even when the vicarage or manse is a superior residence such as the one I have just described, it often goes against the grain to have to live in a 'tied house', especially when thinking about security for the future.

'I'm weary of maintaining, cherishing, and improving other people's houses,' said Mary, herself a vicar's wife of many years' standing. The home is ours, but the house is not—and I think if we are honest most of us would prefer to own our property.

Having said that, I must pay tribute to the many dear Christians who have, in the past, sacrificed a great deal so that I and my family can have somewhere to live. To them we are for ever grateful. When we moved to our first full pastoral charge, a manse had to be purchased, as the previous minister had, in fact, owned his own home. We learnt, many weeks after moving into that place, that one middle-aged man and his wife had given all their holiday savings to help with the purchase, while another, older man had sacrificed all that he had put aside towards a new suit of clothes: 'If the Lord spares me another winter,' he had said, 'he'll provide me with some warm woollies!'—and he did.

Of course, not all clergy live in borrowed houses. Some ministers nowadays are in a position to buy their own property, especially when they are ordained in the mid-stream of their lives. However, it must be said that the salary paid to a 'gentleman of the cloth' does not easily run to paying off a mortgage, so I suppose it is the privileged few who actually do own their homes. Indeed, an Anglican vicar is bound by law to live in the vicarage provided, even though he may own property elsewhere.

The majority of parsonages for Church of England clergy are purpose-built today. Not only does the house have to provide a home for the vicar and his family; it is also his place of work. The Church Commissioners lay down clear guidelines concerning their requirements for suitable houses. The overall floor area should be about 167 square metres (a greater proportion of this to be on the ground floor), allowing space for living and working. Detailed attention is given to maintaining the privacy of the family within the vicarage walls, and providing adequate space, both inside and outside the house, for visitors—including those confined to wheelchairs or pushing babies in prams. The vicar's study should ideally have a floor area of not less than fourteen square metres, and should be in a quiet and private location within the house, not immediately beneath a child's bedroom or next door to a toilet, thus preserving good sound insulation. There must be two self-contained living rooms, with no interconnecting doors or screens, so that a variety of activities can take place simultaneously without encroaching upon each other. There should be four bedrooms, with sleeping space for not less than six people, hand wash-basins in two of these, and fitted wardrobes in at least two also. Many other conditions are laid down in the architect's brief, all designed to help the vicar discharge his responsibility to the parish with minimum fuss, and at the same time live in a measure of privacy and comfort with his family.

Most Free Church Manses, on the other hand, are not purpose-built to help their tenant to function properly. In fact, many seem to be deliberately designed to make his task more difficult! Often they are situated some distance from the church, which makes getting the family there on Sunday mornings quite a problem, since Dad always has to arrive early. Their architecture frequently leaves much to be desired, if the home is to be used for meetings and private consultations.

It is essential to have a separate study, shut away from the rest of the house. In one of the houses we have lived in there was nowhere at all that could be regarded as private. It is not only walls that have ears—little children do too— and they have most effective voices. A minister must have a place where he can be quiet, to commune with his Lord and prepare his spoken ministry, and where people who come to talk over intimate spiritual matters don't feel themselves overheard by the rest of the household.

That particular house was built on an open-plan system, with the stairs leading straight into the living room. We frequently held evening meetings in our home, and it seemed that the children always made a trip to the bath-room during the quieter moments of a prayer time. Of course they never remembered to shut the door! My father calls it 'the happy gurgle of laughing water, having done its duty'—but however we may describe it, such 'music' is probably not the ideal accompaniment to a prayer meeting! Oh, and while on the subject of toilets, one up and one down are a must in a house that regularly plays host to a number of visitors at a time.

'Please thank your daughter for letting us have her room,' was the parting shot of a missionary couple, as they left early one morning having conducted a meeting in our church the previous evening. It was, in fact, the third time that month that Rosalind had slept on a mattress in our room. She didn't complain, but oh, wouldn't it be lovely to have a guest room!

To anyone who is responsible for providing a Free Church Manse, I would say do insist on four bedrooms. Part of our ministry is entertaining, and an extra bedroom over and above the average family requirements is so helpful.

I suppose it goes without saying that a large lounge is also a necessity. This is perhaps the one time that an open-plan house does come into its own. Many times we have used the stairs as an extra gallery to accommodate more people, particularly at YPF squash meetings and the annual Christmas open house. The room must be big enough to hold people as well as furniture. In our very first manse, if more than seven people turned up for a home-based meeting, it was standing room only. Eventually we pushed out the furniture and sat them all on the floor—all right apart from their having to negotiate the furniture in the hall before they could get into the room!

There really should be a garage too. If the house is too small, no doubt the garage will be used as a store for all the things that don't fit indoors, but I mean a garage for keeping the car in. A minister travels many miles visiting, preaching, attending meetings and committees. It costs a great deal to buy and maintain his car. If he can cosset it a little, not leaving it to fend for itself on cold, frosty nights, it will reward him and the church with good service. More than once the minister who lives in my house has been called out in the middle of the night. How much quicker and easier his journey would have been if he had not had to battle with frozen windows and a cold engine before setting off.

I suppose you would expect me to mention the kitchen, being a woman. Should it be large, or should it be small? I have had both. Each has its advantages. Preferably it should be big enough to cater for a crowd occasionally, certainly with enough worktop space to lay out trays of cups and saucers. Beyond that, every woman probably has a dream-kitchen in her mind, but in reality those are generally reserved for people other than clergy wives!

With the help of several friends married to clergymen, I have now consumer-tested quite a number of clerical homes. I think I would give the prize to one that has all the desirable qualities of four bedrooms, a private study, large lounge, upstairs and downstairs toilets, big kitchen, and integral garage. In addition it is within easy reach of the church. Within the course of a week, there is plenty of traffic between church and manse, and a five-minute walk is a comfortable measure between the two. This particular house is also only five minutes from a major shopping area, and even nearer to the children's school, yet is in a quiet residential area, with a pleasant outlook. The garden is manageable, even for reluctant clergy. The house has been well maintained, double-glazed and roof-lagged. In fact, it is almost an estate agent's dream, but I don't think the church will be selling it for a long time. Ministers come and ministers go, and they each add their individual touch which turns the manse into home during their stay. It fits the bill perfectly, and the church is hanging on to it.

5

Time Out

One day I got talking to a lady on the train, and happened to say that my husband was the minister of a church, partly, I must confess, to see what her reaction would be. It was not quite what I had expected: 'Oh, you lucky people,' she exclaimed, 'working a one day week! I've always dreamt of having a job like that—but then, I don't really think that Bible-thumping is quite me....' She then returned to gazing wistfully out of the window.

Perhaps a one-day working week does sound attractive, though I guess we'd find it very unproductive. Ours seems more like an eight-day week usually—and here we come up against a problem.

'Mum, you're such a bore,' my son announced one day. 'You're always working!' He was right. I was a bore, and he had every right to complain. I thought of our Saviour's invitation to his disciples to 'come away...and rest a while' (Mk 6:31), checked the words of martyred justification which were rising to my lips, and took an hour out to walk with him in the local park. We watched a squirrel digging into its winter store of beech nuts, collected frog spawn from the pond, and returned home both relaxed and stimulated. Everybody needs refreshment and recreation, physically speaking. If we had no meals, never sat down or went to bed, none of us would last very long.

As with any other area of our lives, an important word here is 'balance'. Whether referring to doctrinal teaching, interpretation of Scripture, or Christian activity, there is always a need for it. Somebody once said, 'If you get so well-balanced, you'll stand still and make no progress in your Christian life.' I'm not sure that this is true. A properly tuned, upright vehicle will move much more readily and smoothly than one that is tipping off-centre, caught up with side issues.

When it comes to the allocation of our time and energies, we need to pay attention to the needs of our whole personalities, physical and emotional as well as spiritual. I wonder how many Christians have completely burnt out in their endeavour to be busy in the Lord's work, suffering both physical and mental exhaustion. I could name a few.

Sometimes I get the impression that people think there is great merit in having deep spiritual conversations late into the night, or in working long hours without any thought of taking a cat-nap or indulging in some form of recreation. Surely this is not so. God made this marvellous machine, which is my body, in such a way that it needs regular rest and refreshment. There are times when extra demands are made upon it, and at such times he has promised to give the extra strength and support needed, but as a general rule it must abide by its Maker's instructions if it is to function properly.

In a clergyman's home, you could say that he has to find the right balance between church time, family time and rest time. For him, church time will take priority. For his wife, family time will probably head the list. But what about the third category? Often it is left until a 'more convenient season'. A Christian pastor is on duty twenty-four hours a day. Although it is essential that he has time to relax and build up his resources, this is very difficult to do at home, because the phone still rings with emergency calls for help, and people in need still come to the door.

I well remember the year we tried to take a week's holiday at home. The first morning the phone rang quite early, and a voice said, 'I know you are really on holiday, but are you able to help me with this deep problem?' I suppose the short answer should have been, 'Yes, we are; and no, we can't,' but ...!

Later that same week the husband of one of our church members was suddenly called home to be with his Lord. I leave you to guess to whom his widow naturally turned in her time of grief and distress. Of course we were glad to be there when needed, but such occasions do highlight the problems of trying to relax at home.

Before becoming a Free Church minister, Jonathan had held a managerial position in a city office. He worked hard and carried a great deal of responsibility. Occasionally he took work home, but only occasionally. Sometimes he entertained clients to dinner. However, most evenings and weekends were spent in relaxation and Christian fellowship.

A systematic, methodical person by nature, he realized, on entering the ministry, that much of his pastoral visitation would have to take place in the evenings, when people were home from work. Also, of course, he would now have to regard the mid-week meeting on a Tuesday evening as his responsibility, not merely as an opportunity to worship with other Christians and learn from somebody else's ministry. Because of this, it seemed sensible to set aside other time during the week for relaxation.

The first 'day off' that he and his wife endeavoured to enjoy was disastrous! Shortly after the children had left for school, a neighbour's cat jumped in through the kitchen window and half drowned itself in a sinkful of water—left there because the drain had become blocked. Jonathan's wife, Jill, had gone to town to buy a marvellous black rubber gadget—apparently useful in this sort of emergency. On her return home, she found Jonathan on his knees, trying to give artificial respiration to the cat!

'Better phone the vet,' she suggested, and they both made a dash for the yellow pages, up in Jonathan's study. The cat, meanwhile, had had quite enough of this awful house, and, apparently fully recovered, fled to the nether regions of the garden. Jon and Jill emerged from the study, having had no success in raising a vet, only to find the kitchen deserted, and no sign of the ailing puss anywhere.

So they turned their attention to the sink. 'It's quite easy,' said Jonathan, with an air of leave-it-to-me-I-know-what-I'm-doing, and he carefully placed the rubber plunger over the plughole. A quick push and pull; an excruciating gurgle, as though the poor drainpipe was having a severe bout of indigestion, and the water trickled happily away. 'There, I told you it was easy,' he cried. 'I'll just give it another go to make sure all the gunge has gone.' And so saying, he pumped the marvellous gadget with all his might. A fountain of black shiny 'something' shot up into Jonathan's face, and gently ran right down the front of his clean white shirt.

Just at that precise moment the doorbell rang. Jill went running to the door, trying to choke back the mirth caused by her husband's plight, to find a dejected little lady standing there, obviously very near to tears. 'Can I come in a minute, dearie? I'm in such trouble.' And for the next hour they ministered to this poor, hurting soul in her distress.

By midday they felt quite exhausted from coping with each successive crisis, made psychologically greater because in their minds they had thought of this as their day off. Jill had decided not to cook on such days, so they snatched a sandwich, and since the sun was shining stretched out on their loungers in the garden. Jonathan had just dozed off nicely when the side-gate creaked, and a moment later one of his church members appeared round the corner of the house, having failed to get any response to the doorbell. 'So this is what you get up to when our backs are turned!' It was said as a joke, but neither Jon nor Jill were really sure about that at the time.

I suppose that was the beginning of the guilt complex about free time for these two servants of God. They found throughout the following months that whenever they tried to relax during the day time, they felt that they really ought not to. For them, learning to unwind and allowing themselves space to refresh both body and mind was a painful business, and even now, years later, they sometimes feel a twinge of guilt if their lunch hour stretches to an hour and a half, or they take a morning off to stroll around the shops in a leisurely fashion. Occasionally Jon takes his wife out for lunch to give her a break from preparing food, and to give them both an opportunity to enjoy each other's company outside the home. Why is it, I wonder, that they always feel bound to drive several miles away on these occasions, despite the fact that there are a number of good restaurants in their own town? Is it the fear of being discovered? 'What other people might think' probably colours much of what we all do and don't do, but we are rather weak creatures if we can't act with conviction on what we feel to be a right course of action.

For those of us who find ourselves in a position of leadership among the Lord's people, there is a very particular responsibility not to place a stumbling-block in the path of young Christians. They may be watching us for a pattern of so-called Christian behaviour. I am constantly challenged by the words of the Apostle Paul to the believers in Philippi: 'What you have learned and received and heard and seen in me, do' (Phil 4:9). How I wish I could say that to those who look to me for such practical guidance—but I dare not!

Many of the taboos of half a century ago have been lifted I am glad to say, but of course there is always the danger of standards swinging back to an all-time low, so we do need to be constantly on our guard in this, as in all other aspects of life, to maintain the right balance.

During the early days of our ministry, a certain film was showing in a large town twenty miles away. It was acclaimed as an epic, and at the same time good, wholesome stuff! We were not in the habit of going to the cinema, and in fact had been taught to treat it with a great deal of caution. However, the desire to see this film was strong, and as its wholesome entertainment value was highly rated we decided to take time to see it. For some reason—was it fear of being accused of indulging in 'sin'?—we did not broadcast the fact that we intended to go. In the event, we drove to the town in question, but after a protracted and fruitless search for a parking space near the cinema, we gave up and returned home without having seen the film after all!

Somehow the ever-efficient bush-telegraph got hold of the story, but, as usual, it became distorted as it was passed along. A week later it came to our ears that some of the young converts in our church youth group, who had been warned off the cinema by well-meaning older folk, now felt that they had licence to go, because we ourselves had been to see a film of dubious content! Not even the one that we had not seen, if you see what I mean...!

A few years after this event we took fourteen teenagers to Austria for a summer houseparty. It was a long journey since we were driving there in separate cars, so we had arranged to spend two nights in a German *Gasthof* en route. It was a very comfortable, typically German guest house-cum-bar-cum-café. On the Sunday afternoon the youngsters went for a walk, and left us sitting in the garden sipping our lemonade. Shortly after their departure our host appeared, beaming with delight and generosity, carrying a tray with three glasses of whisky—cubes of ice clinking tunefully in each one. He sat at our table, and sought to dispense his hospitality and engage us in conversation, which was quite amusing, since his English matched my German 'O' level variety of ten years' vintage! We wanted to take advantage of the opportunity to share the gospel, as he was most interested in what we were into, and how we had charge of 'such a beautiful group of boys and girls'! In between sips of the forbidden liquor we tried to tell him of the love of Jesus, and how he could transform people's lives; but as the conversation lengthened, we both knew that soon our 'beautiful boys and girls' would be returning from their walk. To see us sitting there, knocking back the hard stuff with a German innkeeper didn't seem quite right somehow!

Mercifully he was called away to the phone, and the rest of the whisky was poured hastily under the table. However, on his return, amid much profuse apology for having had to leave so hurriedly, he noticed the empty glasses, and was most anxious to refill them! Thank goodness we had the presence of mind to request a couple of cokes instead.

That wasn't the end of the story. Next morning, as we prepared to leave, our exceedingly generous host presented us with two large bottles of very superior wine as a parting gift. I don't think he had ever had such a large party of foreigners book into his hostelry before, and was over-flowing with thankfulness. Not only was the wine itself an embarrassment, in front of our protégés, but it exceeded the limit permitted into our country without customs decla-ration! So our next dilemma was whether to declare it, drink it before the journey home, or give a bottle to one of the others to bring in for us. Only three of them were old enough to do so anyway. What a marvellous story it would have made in the local paper: 'Baptist minister inveigles young adults to assist in smuggling alcohol into Britain'—or something equally exaggerated. (Lest such a thing should happen, it seemed prudent to give half the bounty to our Austrian hosts when we left for home a fortnight later. They appreciated it, I know.)

All in all that Austrian holiday proved to be a great benefit to all who came with us. It was an international houseparty, comprising young people from eleven different

countries, including quite a few from Eastern Europe.
They, in particular, made a deep impression on our group.
They didn't talk much about the privations they suffered at
home because of their Christian faith, but something came
over through their personalities of what it means to be 'per-
secuted for righteousness' sake', and how they were proving
the grace of the Lord in remaining true to him, despite
much pressure.

Anna was from Poland. Her father had been a university
lecturer, but was made redundant (with no dole money)
when he would not renounce his Christian beliefs. He
couldn't even get a job sweeping streets or emptying dust-
bins. His name was on the blacklist issued to every conceiv-
able employer. Anna herself was a very gentle, caring girl.
She seemed totally at peace, and full of the joy that only
Jesus gives to those going through deep waters.

Pavel and his Russian wife had come out of another
Eastern European country to that houseparty. He had a
fairly privileged position in his native town, and had not
disclosed his reason for coming on this holiday, which was
to hear more of Christian belief. They had both become
interested through watching the purposefulness displayed
in the lives of Christians they knew. During their time in
Austria they both came to know Jesus for themselves, and
gladly recognized his lordship in their lives, little heeding
the possible consequences on their return home. These and
others made a profound impression on our own young
people whose experience and understanding was considerably broadened.

For a number of years Eddie and I were involved in a
holiday ministry of this kind, in conjunction with the European Christian Mission. It was enormous fun! One year the
rain fell every day for the whole fortnight, and the surrounding mountains never once made an appearance, but
nobody minded. We just went out and got wet, came home
to a hearty Austrian meal of dumpling or noodle soup,

followed by black bread topped with all kinds of cheese and sausage, and then spent the evening singing God's praises in a number of different languages and having Bible study and discussion together. I don't think we have ever laughed so much in one fortnight as we did that year! There was lots of light-hearted banter, often made all the more hilarious by having to juggle with words in little-known languages, which was unavoidable in such a cosmopolitan group.

We ourselves gained a lot from working together in a concentrated effort with a team of ten or twelve, mostly missionaries. It's surprising how close you can become to others in such a short time. We learnt a little of what it must have meant to the early church who 'had all things in common' (Acts 2:44). If we popped into a *Gasthof* for a coffee or a glass of apple juice, anyone who had money in their pocket would pay. Sometimes we found ourselves paying for somebody else, while yet another would pay for us. There was no sense of indebtedness; we all acted as one person! In fact, at the end of one of these memorable houseparties, one young man became a Christian, largely because, he said, 'I have seen here how you believers can laugh and be happy together. Before I always thought you had to be serious and solemn all the time!'

Those experiences expanded our outlook, and established many contacts, which were to be a blessing to our church fellowship back home in time to come. I am convinced that if a minister is given time to engage in some sort of holiday ministry, apart from his own 'real' holiday, his fellowship at home is greatly enriched because of it. Not only did we take a number of our young people on one of our trips to Austria, but several folk whom we met on those occasions later came to minister to our own congregation, bringing with them fresh insight and stimulus.

Our European experience mostly took place before we had children of our own. Since then we have spent a number of summers helping to run a Scripture Union beach mission in Cornwall. Now, having been bitten with the beach mission bug and realizing its potential as a training ground for young believers, as well as its usefulness in actually bringing the gospel to hundreds who would not otherwise hear it, we have been encouraging our teenagers to get involved during their long summer vacations.

Surely, to release one's minister or vicar to engage in such ministry can only bring good to the local church. He won't return home rested, but he will have been greatly stimulated, and packed away within his storehouse of experience will be many little treasures to delight his congregation's heart. The first few summers that we did anything of this kind, we came straight back to the normal routine. It was a mistake. Nowadays we always take at least a week's relaxing holiday immediately following such events, and find that we are far better fitted to taking up the reins again on our return.

Perhaps an even greater 'fellowship-enrichment' results from a minister's more permanent involvement with some other Christian organization. When David had been in his third parish for a couple of years, he was approached by a certain missionary society to become involved in the administration of that mission. As long as he could remember, he had always been keenly interested in the work of this particular mission, but if he were to do the proposed task properly it would take two or three days out of every month, besides giving him an extra weight of responsibility to carry. Already he frequently wished there were thirty-six hours in every day, in order to cope with all the demands which came his way. How could he possibly take on more?

He and his wife, June, decided to make it a matter of enquiring prayer, and it was, in fact, to June that the Lord spoke first. She was preparing ministry to be given at the close of her next Mother's Union meeting, when she came across Isaiah 54:2, 'Enlarge the place of your tent, and let the curtains of your habitations be stretched out; hold not back, lengthen your cords and strengthen your stakes....' Somehow she knew that was God's word at that time for David, but hesitated to show it to him immediately. She went to the Mother's Union, and gave her brief epilogue at the close of the meeting. As the women were gathering their things to go, June stood reaching up to a high shelf to replace a book, when a small voice at her elbow (she is very tall) suddenly said, 'I'd like a word with you, Mrs Stratton, about those "lengthened cords".' June turned to see little Mrs Silver, a dear soul whom she knew to be a very prayerful woman. 'I think God has told me that it is time you and Vicar lengthened yours a bit, you know. I don't really know what it's all about, but you are getting a bit cramped in this church, and when you read that verse just now, he said to me: "Julia, you go and tell that young woman that those lengthened cords are for her and her dear hubbie." So here I am dear. I'm sure you'll get the message right!'

And so it was that David became first a committee member, and later the chairman of that particular Christian mission. He didn't know then that because of his personal involvement four of the young people in his parish would eventually spend their lives serving the Lord under its umbrella—but that's how it was to be! And again, as with our holiday ministry, the time he spent on a whistle-stop tour of the mission field, his added knowledge of what the Lord is doing in other parts of the world, and the occasional visits to his church of men and women working with the mission, have altogether enriched his own ministry and the experience of his listeners.

I suppose that it could be considered by some to be unproductive to have a finger in a number of pies. I have even heard it said in some circles, where the minister's salary is paid entirely by the local church fellowship, that the people who pay that salary should have the man's total commitment. Why should they pay him to give his time to another organization? This seems to me to be a very short-sighted observation. Experience shows that a pastor's involvement with such things as missionary activities and holiday ministry reaps rich dividends for his home congregation.

In the beginning, when God created this world, he instituted a rest on the seventh day. Later he ordained such a Sabbath for the good of the land every seven years. In his economy, the principle of rest and recuperation seems to pertain to all living things. The idea of taking a sabbatical is one which has gained increasing popularity among the clergy in recent years, and has been used by many to great advantage.

Peter had been in the Baptist ministry for fifteen years, and was aware that the content of his weekly preaching would be much richer if only he could spend more time in the study. However, as the pastoral demands increased and, with a growing congregation, the administration also piled up, study time was becoming less, rather than more! Who it was that first suggested he take time out for concentrated reading, he was never sure—but the idea grew, and his elders encouraged him to make it a priority. He was offered the use of a holiday flat, out of season, and also of somebody's second car. So it was that one wet Monday in February he set off for his temporary home; the car boot stacked with all the books he had been intending to read for the past X number of years, plenty of file-paper and a tin-opener. It was just as well that he was not on his way to Roy Plumley's desert island, I don't think he would have found it possible to choose just one of those precious study books!

The following four months proved to be some of the most stimulating and refreshing in the whole of his ministry. To soak himself in God's word without constantly being on the lookout for sermon material; to have time to think an issue through from start to finish without frequent interruptions from the telephone bleep, filled him with a new kind of restfulness and accomplishment. He discovered the joy of private worship in such a way as he had never known before. On Sundays he visited a number of different churches, and really enjoyed being on the receiving end of somebody else's ministry. Every alternate weekend his wife and family joined him, and how they too appreciated going together to worship the Lord, something which they had not done throughout their marriage, except for the odd Sunday during holiday times.

When Peter returned to his own church fellowship later that Spring, he felt like a new man—and everyone else noticed the difference too! For Jane, his wife, it had not been a particularly easy time with two growing children to care for, and the added responsibility in home and church life, but she too learnt much from the exercise. Peter rang her two or three times a week, and she laughingly said that they made more time to talk together during those four months than when he was at home. In actual fact, Jane discovered a gift of gentle authority in counselling matters, which she had not been aware of in herself before, having always left the heavy ones to Peter! The elders of their church looked after her very well. Having always felt that the church members held her a little apart because of her position as Peter's wife, she was surprised to find how much they cared, and that she really did belong after all. Maybe some of her 'loneliness' in previous years had been self-imposed!

Michael's sabbatical took quite a different form. One of the issues he had wanted to get to grips with for a long while was an in-depth study of church growth. News had reached his ears of a phenomenal burst of life in Christian fellowships in various parts of the world, and he longed to investigate. Then his attention was drawn to a six-week course on the subject to be held in an American seminary. After giving the matter much prayer and thought, he decided to take two and a half months out to enrol in this course of study and to spend a month with friends in America. They very kindly fixed up some preaching engagements for him during that month which helped considerably in financing the trip!

Like Peter, he benefited greatly from the change of scene, as well as the actual course of study. On his return his own parishioners caught his enthusiasm to put into practice many of the principles which he had learnt, and are still thriving on the experience.

It was under 'Forthcoming Attractions' in a church magazine from the West of England that the following entry appeared: 'The vicar will be away from the parish for the first three weeks of the coming month.' I hope that the vicar's absence is not normally considered to be a 'forthcoming attraction', but time out from the daily round and common task is something we all need. Give your 'shepherd' a roving commission, and he will find the most lush pasture available for his 'sheep'. Allow him time and opportunity to refresh himself, and he will be more able to lovingly tend his 'flock'.

6

Children or Church—Which Comes First?

'Mummy, I think I've got the centre of gravity. Look, look, Mum....' It was a do-it-yourself submarine under construction. Before I had made the full naval inspection of this great masterpiece, another voice assailed my ears:

'What is forty-three, divided by six? I can't make it go. It's not fair, I can never do it....'

I was actually trying to write a stimulating article for the church magazine at the time, but finding the task quite impossible, especially when, a few moments later, the smell of burning reached my nostrils, reminding me of a cake which should have been removed from the oven twenty minutes ago.

No doubt this sort of thing happens in many homes; also in vicarage and manse families! They are not immune to argument and problems among themselves, either, surprising though that may seem to some. The children squabble like other kids do. They are surrounded by worldly influences, just like other kids are. They have the same hopes and aspirations as other children, the same uncertainty about future employment, the same pressures to do well, and alongside all this, they are also expected by a large number of people to be super-kids where behaviour and spiritual fervour are concerned.

Of course the minister's son will always be at the Youth Fellowship, and yes, he will take the opening prayer, and give the talk too if necessary. His dad is the minister, after all, and it would be a pretty poor show if he didn't support the youth group!

'It's a pity,' I once heard someone say. 'She used to be a pretty little thing, but now he lets her put paint on her fingernails, and she even wears trousers in church! I'm surprised at our vicar. You'd think he'd be more careful about his own daughter.'

As a mum in a manse, I often feel as though parishioners' eyes are focused on me and my family, noticing how we bring them up and what we allow them to do, and passing judgement accordingly.

'You are not strong enough with your boy. He ought to be in church on Sunday evenings.' At least it was said to my face, so I could defend my decision to allow our twelve-year-old son the freedom to come with us to church, or not, as he wished. I would far rather that he missed out for a year or two then, and chose to come himself at a later age, than be forced to attend while young, and be frightened off for evermore. I have met too many people, not necessarily from ministers' homes, who suffered three services a day throughout their childhood, and have since, to use their words, 'given up on religion' because it seemed irrelevant and boring.

A service of worship designed for mature adults is not going to grab a child who particularly dislikes singing, and whose real interest is model railways and chemical experiments. Prayer plays an important part in his home life, Covenanters is super, the Lord is consulted on every decision, but church just does not meet his needs at the moment. It is a shame about the singing, but who said that a Christian minister's children must be musical? Or, for that matter, tidy and well-spoken, thoughtful and polite? All these things we hope for and encourage in our children, but they weren't born angels, and they have to develop, just like others.

Sometimes I feel that children of the manse are under particular pressure. It might even be called spiritual attack. Here is their dad, in a position of leadership within the body of Christ. 'Bring him down,' thinks the Enemy of souls, 'and the cause of Christ will suffer.'

Maybe Dad is pretty good at wielding the Spirit's sword, and daily wears the armour of God instead of leaving it hanging neatly in Ephesians 6. So what does the Enemy do? He'll more than likely get at the children. They are far more vulnerable, especially if Mum and Dad are busy with all the parishioners' upsets and problems.

Which brings me to a big drum I feel I must beat loudly. If God gives a vicar and his wife a family, those children really should take priority whenever conflict arises between claims of church and home. Maybe the responsibility for this rests more on the wife's shoulders. I guess that is why I feel so strongly about it. Many spiritual casualties in ministers' families (not all) have been caused by their parents being too busy in their formative years. Our child is a gift from God. He has entrusted us to care for that child, to train him and lead him into adult life. We are the only two parents he will ever have, and we must take the responsibility seriously.

When the apostle Paul wrote to young Timothy listing the qualities required in a church leader, he did not mince matters where that leader's domestic responsibility was concerned: 'He must manage his own family well and see that his children obey him with proper respect. (If anyone does not know how to manage his own family, how can he take care of God's church?)' (1 Tim 3:4–5, New International Version.) 'Proper respect' has to be earned; it is not a parent's automatic right. To gain it there must be, on our side, a big input of time and love.

Recently I received a letter from some missionary friends

in India. One phrase in particular has stuck in my mind: 'Pray that we will find quality time to spend with our boys.' What is quality time? It is not long hours and expensive outings. It is ten minutes total listening time just before bed, or whenever they seem to require it. It is an evening walk together by the river, or perhaps a game of ball in the back garden.

When Rosalind, our daughter, was much younger, an arm fell off a favourite doll. I really did intend mending it, but somehow my days became filled with 'far more important things', and despite her repeated requests, it was almost a fortnight before the simple matter was attended to. Do our children sometimes get the message that other people are more important to us than they are? It is 'quality time' that is such a rare, but essential, commodity; time when we can give our undivided attention, making them feel that they matter to us more than anything and anyone else. This is not training them to be selfish; it is teaching them something of their personal worth.

Pam and Ron are not in the ministry, but their church commitment plays a very important role in their lives. He is a churchwarden, and she a Bible class leader. They have three children, two of whom are teenagers, all of whom are lively company. The first time I called at their home, I was left in the room for five minutes with Ruth, then aged three, to await her mother.

'Well now, Auntie, do you know the Lord Jesus?' she asked as she squatted on the floor at my feet, and lifted wide questioning eyes to my face. She seemed totally satisfied with my answer, and moved onto the next important topic of conversation:

'Do you like chocolates? Because if you do, I'll let you have one of Mummy's!' She kept me well entertained until Pam arrived, showing off her favourite toys and books, and letting me hold her pet hamster. She is now eleven years old and, like her older brother and sister, can still hold a sparkling conversation.

Despite the busyness of Mum and Dad, this family always strikes me as being how a Christian family ought to be. There are disagreements and squabbles from time to time, but the children have absolutely no hang-ups or odd quirks of behaviour. They very obviously enjoy each other's company and being with their parents. There seems to be no big divide between one generation and the other. Somebody once asked Pam how she managed to produce such happy kids. Her answer was: 'Sheer hard work!'

I do know, however, that she and Ron have prayed daily for their children, about the friendships they make, about the discipline they themselves exercise within the home, about the family's spiritual welfare. They have prayed regularly, even since before birth, about each one's future partner in life too!

As it happens, they have no television set in their home. No doubt this has promoted the art of conversation, though some would possibly feel that they have been somewhat deprived because of it! When Pam and Ron relax, the whole family relaxes. They actually do things together, and always have done. For the last two summers the two older children have helped on a Beach Mission team in Cornwall. They have been attending that particular Beach Mission since they were both in nappies. The whole family goes every year. They all have a whale of a time, and number three, young Ruth, can't wait to get 'on the team'.

Even in Christian circles, to see a family as well-integrated as this one is a rare sight. So what about those whose wheels don't grind so smoothly?

Joanne was in a girls' Bible class which I used to lead. She had first come to church in her pram, and had attended Sunday School for as long as she could remember. Her home was one where family prayers were regular, and where all the standards practised were based on Bible teaching.

When she was in her early teens, she 'went forward' at an evangelistic meeting, and we were all thrilled to see her new enthusiasm for the Lord. She was a bright, attractive, bubbly girl, always good fun to have around, and easily talked about how real Jesus had become to her.

On leaving school she moved away from home to start training for her chosen career, but her hopes of finding a lively church fellowship, and friends to match, were not realized. She very soon became open to a number of temptations and influences, which until then she had not realized existed!

Her enthusiasm for the Lord Jesus cooled considerably, and her new friends introduced her to what seemed an exciting new world. For a while she worked as a 'bunny-girl' at Mayfair's Playboy Club. Later she spent a summer hostessing on private yachts, sailing round the Med, frequently hobnobbing with the rich and famous, and, seemingly, far from God.

It spelt heartache for those of us who had watched her grow up into the Lord's love, especially for Mum and Dad. But we were reminded of the prodigal son's father in Luke 15, who let his son go...and we held on in prayer.

Eventually, like that boy, Joanne 'came to an end of herself', and found her way back to her Saviour, who welcomed her gladly. Today she is a delightful young mother, and together with her husband leads a youth group in her local church. No doubt her own experience enables her to help many other youngsters who are finding the worldly pressures almost too much to bear.

Perhaps her story can serve as some encouragement to Christian parents whose hearts are being torn apart by errant sons and daughters. Joanne's 'sojourn in the far country' lasted just a few years. Some parents have been nursing a heartache for much longer than that, and still can't see any light at the end of the dark tunnel. For them there is a constant cry nagging at the back of their minds:

'Where did we go wrong?'

Let us remind ourselves that at the end of the day our children have to make their own decisions about following the Lord Jesus Christ. They are still 'their own people', and although a Christian family heritage is invaluable, they cannot take over a second-hand faith!

'Where did we go wrong?' is probably the wrong question to ask. I am sure that sometimes some of us did go wrong; applied too much pressure to make a spiritual response, perhaps; exercised too much or not enough discipline; tried too hard to squeeze them into our ideal mould, instead of allowing them to develop individually. Oh, there must be a hundred and one ways in which we might have 'gone wrong'. But nonetheless I do believe that we can do absolutely nothing towards healing the situation, if we hold ourselves entirely responsible for the waywardness of our offspring, and sit wallowing in despair. When they were small, they fell in happily with everything we deemed necessary for their spiritual and moral education. Now they have grown up, and are expressing their individuality. Instead of bewailing: 'Where did we go wrong?' let us put the emphasis on: 'What can we do to restore them?'

One thing I am convinced about is the power of prayer within this context. For one thing, if I am praying earnestly about my straying child, I am continually assured of the Lord's care for that child, which helps me in my acceptance of the situation. Until I can accept that my child has a right to rebel, I am too biased to give much constructive help. To know that my Lord really cares, and can still touch my child, despite that rebellion, helps me enormously. So when I stretch out my hand in his or her direction, it will be stretched out in love, not judgement.

I have a friend who came to know Jesus in middle life. She had been raised in a happy, secure Christian home. For many years I knew her aged mother, who prayed for her daughter daily, and always had done. It was not until after her death that that old lady's prayers were answered in the way she so much desired, but I do remember her whispering to me a few days before she went Home: 'Janet's in his hands. I know it.' The peacefulness in her face confirmed her words of assurance. Janet is now a Sunday School teacher, helping other people's sons and daughters to know the Lord Jesus. Her mother would be thrilled if she knew. Perhaps she does!

At the time when she became a Christian, Janet's own son was in his teens. She and three other mums got together and covenanted to pray their children through the teenage years. Every Tuesday, at some time during the day, each mother would be down on her knees, bringing before the Lord her own child and those belonging to her three friends. They kept each other informed as to the immediate needs, and often prayed each other through particular crises. Not only did the young people benefit, but their mothers too had a very special bond between them as a result.

These days we often hear of the 'extended family', in terms of offering hospitality and friendship to those who haven't a family of their own. Some months ago, an elderly lady in our church fellowship said to me: 'Tell me how I can pray for your two children. I feel that the Lord wants me to pray for them both regularly.' And already she has, in this invisible way, helped them through the crises of exams and changing schools. Her prayers have borne fruit, and she herself has derived much joy from being in partnership with our family in this way. I am sure that many other people, especially those who feel alone, could profitably think about extending their family to include the children of their Christian friends in a special bond of prayer. Our children need the support of loving, caring, Christian 'aunts and uncles'. It's a great big, noisy world out there! You and I, on our knees in a quiet place, can do much to love them through the growing years.

Perhaps one of the biggest difficulties for parents today is appreciating the atmosphere in which our children are growing up. This is the television age, when young minds are stimulated and laid bare to adult ideas much earlier than was the case in our childhood. In some respects this is a great improvement on things as they used to be. However, I can't help feeling that in other areas our youngsters are imbibing standards which war against happy family life and good social behaviour. A high proportion of so-called entertainment, centres around the marriage bed defiled, and the yardstick by which immature minds measure acceptable behaviour is decidedly short of Bible-based standards.

Then, turning from the media to the world of work, we see people demanding pay-rises on every hand, refusing to work if such increases are not forthcoming. Our children learn that if you want something which your elders are none too eager to give you, just keep shouting, 'I want it,' stick your heels in, and eventually they will give way! Grown-ups do it. It must be right.

All children in Western society are exposed to these things, and for those from Christian homes there are added pressures: 'Richard, you can't seriously think that the world was made by some invisible God! Nobody believes that nowadays. Science disproved it long ago....' And in Richard's mind a little seed of doubt is sown. Mum and Dad seem pretty convinced, but perhaps they are a bit out of date after all. The science teacher should know about that kind of thing!

Then there is the school playground; no shortage of ammunition there! The sceptics outnumber the believers by an overwhelming majority, and not all the products of Christian homes have the heart of Daniel when facing today's 'lions'. School life can be very lonely. The taunts and jeers of other kids, and sometimes teachers too, the loose moral standards which are accepted by today's society, the constant barrage of advertising, tempting them to want more and more of this world's goods, all seem to gang up against the child from a Christian home.

When they come home from school, sounding off their theories on occultism or astrology or evolution, why behave like so many ostriches surrounded by desert? It is no good saying 'that's all wrong', unless we can show them why we feel it is wrong. It must be part of a parent's duty to become familiar with what our children are learning, and to know why we believe what we believe, and why we behave how we behave. So often our child will see one set of standards practised at home, and a completely different scale of values at school and among his friends. Unless he wants to be singled out as an object of ridicule, it is much easier to conform to the ways of his peers. So the whole thing boils down to the quality of relationship between himself and his mum and dad. That will determine where his loyalties lie, and that relationship is less likely to be a good one if the family does not come at the top of his parents' priority list where time and interest are concerned.

A group of boys were skulking behind the cycle sheds sharing a cigarette. Tim just happened to walk by at that moment, on his way to the lost property office. He was always losing things! He could not help seeing what his friends were up to.

'Hey, Holy Joe, come and share a fag!'

'No thanks.'

'Why not, Chicken? Won't Daddy let you, eh? Fancy 'aving a dad what's a vicar, then!'

Tim was fed up with the constant jibes about his father's vocation. He was frequently the butt of classroom jokes, not because of his own stand as a Christian (as a matter of fact, at that particular time he had not yet made his child-hood understanding of Christian belief a matter of personal faith), but merely because his father was the school chaplain.

Some vicars' sons would probably have capitulated to the

majority, but what saved the day for Tim was the close relationship that had developed between him and his dad. Since his earliest memories they had spent as much time as possible together. In the pre-school years, he had quite often accompanied his father on pastoral visits, enjoying the car-ride, and the sweets and biscuits frequently proffered by the elderly parishioners whom they were visiting!

In more recent times, Dad was usually out at some committee or other during the evenings, but sometimes he would be home when Tim got back from school. In the summer they would go over to the recreation ground for an hour, and kick a ball about together. In the winter they were frequent visitors to the local model shop and spent quite a bit of time with heads together over the workbench at home. It was good for Dad to be able to relax for a bit in the midst of pressure, and certainly these after-school together-times cemented the relationship between father and son, which was to bear much fruit in later years.

One day our daughter came home, very excited because she had been chosen to swim for her school at the County Gala. This was a high honour, one she had been trying to attain for a long time. We were pleased for her.

'You will come and watch me, won't you?'

'Yes, of course, dear.'

'I said you'd probably help with transport. Miss James will need another car, because there are six of us going.'

'Yes, we'd love to.'

We were always anxious to support the school whenever possible. Keeping on good terms with 'the powers that be' had paid off in the children's junior school days. Whenever we had an evangelistic mission in our church, the headmistress had been only too willing to allow us time in school assembly. On a personal level, too, there had been many opportunities for Christian witness when accompanying a school trip to London, or helping at an open evening. Supporting the school fund raffle, or the cheese and wine evening, might not be 'up our street', but running the swimming team to their gala competition we would be glad to do!

'You might not though!' she said, with some temerity in her voice.

'Oh, why not?'

'It's on Sunday!'

It was like a sudden downpour of rain, completely blotting out the bright sunlight. No, we might not, indeed! Certainly Dad wouldn't be able to help. He had other defined duties on Sundays. Me? Well, I suppose I could go, but it raised questions. What about Rosalind herself? Was this the sort of thing that good Christians don't do on Sundays?

In recent years an increasing number of events, which were once Saturday prerogatives, have been moved to the first day of the week. To draw a line between permissible and non-permissible activities would be a very bold endeavour since so many practising Christians have differing opinions on the subject. In my childhood a great deal of emphasis was put upon the things we don't do on Sundays. Actually our time was well filled with going to church and mealtimes, since Sunday School was always held in the afternoon, and the Christian family was expected to attend both morning and evening worship too. As people have become more aware of the value of family time within the Christian home, most churches have adapted their Sunday programme to leave the afternoons free, but inevitably this has made space for some of the unmentionables!

On the negative side, I suppose the best rule of thumb is: 'If it doesn't interfere with my regular Sunday pursuits, i.e. church service, Bible class, Sunday School, etc., do it!' Why ban a football match if it is considered OK to go for a walk? Why not watch a television play, if I would otherwise happily read an entertaining novel? Why consider that gardening is out, but cooking and washing up in? In the code of Sunday conduct which some of us have lived by, there are lots of dichotomies, and it was not until I had growing children of my own who began to say, 'Why not?' that I realized how stupid some of my rules had been. Gradually I am letting go. I hope I'm not slipping! Sunday should be a day of glad worship, happy Christian fellowship, and rest from the daily round and common task.

On the positive side we try to make it a very special day. Croissants for breakfast, and real cream on the Sunday pud. When the children were little, I kept some games and books which were only used on Sundays. Sunday best clothes are not as much appreciated as they once were, but they too serve to accentuate the special nature of this day.

Sunday in a manse is always fraught with a certain amount of tension. Dad is bound to be preoccupied with the burden of preaching. Perhaps some of his congregation think that he just stands up there and it all flows out, but most know that it is not like that at all. Many hours have gone into study and preparation during the week, and this is the day when that hard work has to stand its test. He is conscious of being God's mouthpiece, and that is a heavy responsibility. His people are anxious to be spiritually fed, and he equally anxious to provide them with a nourishing diet. In between it all, many people there have very personal needs, and they look to him for help and encouragement. He is trying hard to notice who is not present. People feel hurt when they are not missed.

These pressures are felt by the children too, but, certainly during the tender years, are not understood by them. So often it falls to Mother to make it a meaningful day of rest and worship for her family, while shielding her otherwise preoccupied spouse from their excessive boisterousness. Quite a tall order, but a challenge to her ingenuity!

There was a time when we regularly invited members of our fellowship round for Sunday tea, until the family reaction was summed up in: 'Not visitors again!' So it doesn't happen quite so often now. We have had some super Sunday afternoons though, my children and I. Swinging and sliding in the local park, sledging in the winter, collecting conkers and blackberries in the autumn, chasing butterflies and searching for birds' nests in the spring, sailing Jonathan's model boat on the river nearby. He even took his old mum out in a rowing boat one Sunday last summer. It's great to have time to actually be with our children, doing something together which we all enjoy.

There is no doubt that in all Christian families, particularly clergy homes, there does sometimes arise a conflict of commitment where church and children are concerned. It seems to me, however, that when the family commitment is properly fulfilled, the conflict is not nearly so obvious. As a Christian mum, and one whose husband must be at all the church meetings, I accept that my place is in the home. For a little while I will miss the evening service, and the mid-week meeting, and the special events, but it is only for a few years. After that, even if my children do kick over the traces for a bit, I shall know that I have not neglected them during their formative years, and I can trust God's promise: 'Teach a child how he should live, and he will remember it all his life' (Prov 22:6, Good News Bible).

7

People on Our Doorstep

It was late. All the lights in the vicarage had been switched off, except in one upstairs room. Margaret's husband was away at a conference for a few days. She had worked through a busy day, culminating in a somewhat difficult committee meeting held in her home, which had gone on long past bedtime. The presence of other people in the house throughout the evening had made the children restless, but at last they had settled to sleep. As Margaret wearily undressed herself ready for bed, she wondered rather absently if they would wake easily in time for school the next morning, and if that awkward committee member would even now be regaling her husband with her account of the highly-charged meeting.

She sat on the edge of her bed, and reached for her Bible. Suddenly her thoughts were snatched away by a frantic ringing of the doorbell. Whoever could it be at this time of night? For a moment she hesitated. You do hear of awful things happening these days. If only Martin were here! The doorbell continued to sound its alarm.

With a hasty prayer for protection and wisdom to deal with whatever awaited her, Margaret threw on her dressing gown, and hurried downstairs. On the doorstep stood three little children clinging tightly to their mother. Margaret had seen her in church a few times, but didn't know her name.

They stood, red-eyed and dejected, a pathetic little group.

'Come in,' said Margaret, trying to collect her thoughts, and take in the situation.

Once seated in the vicarage lounge, the whole story of their plight came flooding out. Three hours ago the woman's husband had apparently gone berserk, lashing out at his wife and children, and had driven them from the house. Afraid to return, they had walked the streets until now, not knowing what to do. On finding themselves outside the vicarage, the mother realized that here was a place where she could find refuge. The light shining in an upstairs window gave her courage to ring the doorbell.

Margaret's weariness had vanished. In its place there was a compelling reminder of some words of scripture she had read quite recently: 'Inasmuch as you have done it unto one of the least of these, my brethren, you have done it unto me.' She could not remember which gospel writer had recorded these words of Jesus, but she knew exactly what she had to do.

The first thing was to fill the kettle. Warm drinks all round and a mild sedative for Mum; extra blankets from the airing cupboard, and a cuddle for each of the children, all helped to settle the little family down for the night. The two smallest ones slept top to tail on Margaret's settee. They had never done such a thing before, and even that small detail brought a little pleasure into their bruised lives.

They shared Margaret's home for two more days. It was a traumatic time, and eventually their situation was sorted out for the time being. There would, no doubt, be many difficulties for a long while to come. Domestic strife lies at the root of much of the pastoral counselling needs which a clergyman is called in to deal with. Sometimes the answer to the problem is obvious. Often it is not. Sometimes the people involved learn from the experience, making sure that the same area of difficulty does not arise again. Usually they do not.

When Michael and Jean were in their second parish, in a notorious inner city area, they were so beset with ongoing domestic problems among their parishioners, that they almost backed out of the ministry altogether. Time after time they gave of themselves at great sacrifice, only to see all their efforts crumble to nothing. Having very little Christian fellowship in that place, just the two of them would give one day a week to fasting and prayer over some of these difficult situations. There were no apparent results! It hurt inside. They came under severe spiritual attack. Doubt and disillusion clouded their faith.

Then one day a couple, whose marriage had been a stormy affair and for whom Michael and Jean had prayed for many months, suddenly and individually accepted the Lord Jesus Christ as their personal Saviour. It had happened at a big city crusade.

Their love and respect for each other was totally restored. Their whole lifestyle changed into something attractive and joyous. They asked Michael to allow them to remake their marriage vows in a public church service. Their home became a centre for receiving hurting people, and ministering to their needs in a very practical way. Michael and Jean themselves received a 'fresh wind' from the Lord, and realized too that the dark days of frustrated praying had taught them both some precious lessons.

A great deal of a minister's life is spent in encouraging people through their difficulties.

'People don't have problems. People are problems.' Our college lecturer on 'pastoralia' always began his lecture with these words. I am 'people'. You are 'people'. Out there are millions of other 'people'. A few of them will find their way into my home, or yours, because even people outside of church life seem to know enough of the Christian ethic to expect the church to provide help when they need it.

One of my friends lives on a main trunk road connecting

the north of England with London and the south. Her husband is a country parson, and their home is in a fairly small village. The first time she opened her door to a 'Gentleman of the Road', her heart stood still. She knew about these tramps who seemed to spend their lives in transit between one place and another, and had even seen them from time to time when travelling herself, but never before had she actually spoken to one.

She was quite surprised when he spoke clearly and politely. His request left her standing for a few moments: could she give him some work to do please? No, she couldn't really. It was late in the day, so could she suggest somewhere for him to spend the night? No, she didn't know anywhere at all.

She had always thought that a sandwich and a mug of tea at the back door was all that was required on these occasions—but she didn't offer it, all the same. She was sorry. She couldn't help. He'd have to try elsewhere.

He hung his head, and plodded away down the garden path, his pathetic little plastic bag of belongings dangling from his elbow. She felt dreadful!

So began a spate of such callers. She now has a list of sheltered accommodation fixed up near the front door, and another of local employers who sometimes take short-term workers. Over recent years she has come to recognize a few of the regular visitors. In some cases her initial fear has almost been turned to affection!

Strangely enough, her husband is rarely at home when these people call, and she almost always has to deal with them alone. Occasionally she feels she has been taken for a ride, particularly when persuaded to part with a five pound note 'for a good hot meal and a night's kip, Mrs'. Some of them, no doubt, do think that the church is a soft touch, and exploit the vicar or his wife for their own ends. But in among those, there are the genuine cases of need, and my friend is anxious not to turn them away wanting. Perhaps whenever anyone appears at our door asking for help, our immediate thought should be: 'What would Jesus do?', and act according to his example.

Another clergy wife always invites her 'roadies' into the house, no matter how dirty or dishevelled their appearance. She sits them down in a comfortable chair, close to the fire in winter, and provides a hot meal on a tray. She has even been known to make up a camp bed in the church hall on occasions. To her it is a joy to give a little bit of comfort and pleasure to an otherwise drab and miserable life. She also keeps a cupboard of secondhand men's clothing, and has never yet met a refusal when offering any of the goodies from this collection. This is part of her ministry for the Lord, and she never regards 'travellers' as a threat or a nuisance.

Not all people in need of counselling or practical help come from outside the bounds of the church fellowship, and not all come calling on the doorstep. More and more in these days, we are being made aware of deep hurts within the lives of many church members. Sometimes such wounds bear physical consequences as well as emotional scars. A broken home, an unhappy childhood and upsets within marriage have themselves been the catalyst which has brought many to Christ. They have become Christians, but that does not mean their past problems or personality clashes are instantly wiped away. Often the source of emotional pain has to be worked through, and this can take weeks, months or even years in some cases.

Sue is a mother with teenage children. A few years ago her husband's employment took them many miles away from the town where they had both grown up, and despite settling into a happy church fellowship quite quickly, it was a while before she really felt at home in her new surroundings. Coming from a very open, friendly community, Sue and John invited Christian friends into their home, and let it be known that 'Welcome' was written all over their doormat. Gradually people began to take advantage of this open door, until eventually it was a rare thing for an evening to go by without somebody calling, just to share fellowship, or sometimes to unburden themselves concerning some anxiety or other.

Sue realized that a number of people were seeking her out, specifically to share their problems. She wanted to help, and on several occasions was conscious of the Lord's power coming upon her in a particular way to give wise counsel and an understanding concern. Was God calling her into a specific ministry within the local church? Yes, she believed he was. She talked it over with her minister. They prayed about it together, and the conviction grew that this was indeed the Lord's leading. Just as another would be called and equipped to teach a Sunday School class or lead a study group, so Sue was being led into a counselling ministry.

In some people's eyes this area still lies very much within the job-description of the 'professional'—the vicar or minister. In some people's eyes he should be well-versed in all kinds of legal matters, psychological therapy and many other fields of specialized knowledge. Some seem to think that his words of wisdom are the only ones that count for anything! Which reminds me of George.

George was an elderly Christian who had been house-bound for some years. He lived alone, and was looked after by a number of people on the caring team of our church. One day, at the close of a visit to him, I suggested, as usual, that we pray before parting. 'No thanks,' he said, 'not this time. Your old man needn't think he can slide out of coming to see me by sending you. He can pray better too!'

In my experience, there have been several Georges, both male and female, who regard the minister's visits and his prayers rather like a doctor's prescription: without his signature, and his alone, it is not valid! No doubt, spiritual counselling is a specialized subject, and it definitely does come under the umbrella of the minister's work. In most church fellowships nowadays though, the workload in this area is a very heavy one. Usually each case is, on its own, very time consuming, and in a church membership of, say, two hundred people, it is obvious that such a workload has to be shared if it is to be dealt with at all. People like Sue are absolutely necessary.

In some churches, an eldership is appointed on a biblical basis to cope with this sort of thing. Not all of those elders will have the time or opportunity to train themselves for the task. The clergyman was called into the ministry and trained to do the job. The counsellor, likewise, will be called and gifted by God with spiritual discernment, but where it is possible to obtain training to do the job, that is just another part of the Lord's equipment, and should be gladly accepted.

Katie is the wife of a Church of England curate. She has been through a Bible College training, and in the course of that training, learnt quite a bit about caring for people's spiritual and emotional needs. However, she finds that she is much happier speaking at a women's meeting, or teaching a Bible class, than in sitting down on a one-to-one basis with somebody's problem. It seems as though she usually thinks of the words of wisdom long after the needy person has departed! It took time for her to come to terms with this. 'After all,' she reasoned, 'I really ought to be able to help these people. Why do I always feel so tongue-tied and numb in my brain whenever they are here? She even admitted to pangs of jealousy when she discovered another young wife in the church who seemed to always have just the right words to say to a hurting soul.

After a bit Katie realized that her own special gift was respected and appreciated by the people she taught, and her sense of worth became more balanced. Strangely enough, she found that after she had sorted this out in her mind, she became much more relaxed when having to give spiritual counsel to others. 'If the Lord sends them to me,' she said, 'I find now that he often does show me what to say or how to help. Sometimes I am completely nonplussed, and then I can pass them on to somebody else. Always I pray with the person in need, and that really helps them— and me too!'

One Sunday evening I was about to put my children to bed when a knock at the door announced the arrival of a young couple from our church, recently married, both keen, active Christians. I could see that Jenny was upset, and as she sat down in our lounge the tears flowed freely. We let them do so for a few minutes. Then she wiped her eyes and told her tale:

'Nobody understands!' she said. 'I've decided I shall have to give up my Sunday School class. I really can't do it properly with teaching full time and running the home. It takes me ages to prepare my school lessons and mark books. I just can't do Sunday School too. But all the church people think I'm letting them down!'

Poor Jenny! We talked about 'all the church people', who in reality were the two or three to whom she had spoken about the matter, and how perhaps she had misread what they said, or did not say. How often, when under pressure, we misunderstand what others are trying to convey! We talked about school and their new home. Jenny smiled again. I made some coffee and, leaving her and her husband to enjoy it together, went upstairs to tuck my daughter into bed.

'Why was Jenny crying?' she wanted to know. I explained briefly.

'Well, what stupid people to tell her that! I don't expect they would want to work in the Sunday School themselves.'

I think that Rosalind, despite her limited experience of the ways of the world, had hit the nail right on its head. Young, newly-married couples should never be expected to get deeply involved in church work until at least a year after their wedding. Their lives are full enough with work

and home-making. They need time to adjust, to be together, to build their home, to relax and be renewed. By all
means let them enjoy Christian fellowship with other like-
minded people, and use their home to entertain non-Chris-
tian friends. Teaching Sunday School, leading a youth
group and such like responsibility needs commitment of
time and energy, of which newly-weds don't have sufficient
to spare. Why had Jenny taken on the Sunday School class in
the first place? Because she was willing, didn't realize the
pressure it would bring, and others who had the time and
ability were not so willing!

Perhaps some of us have lost the meaning of the biblical
picture of the church as 'the body of Christ'. It implies that
each member of that body has an important part to play if
the whole body is to survive and function properly. Most of
our churches carry too many passengers, members who are
paralysed when it comes to making some personal contribution to the life of the local fellowship, or worse still, who
are constantly criticizing and crippling the activities of other
members of the body. We have, of course, to accept these
people in love. I don't think it would be possible to survive
in the Christian ministry without a generous supply of tact
and tolerance!

David was in the midst of preparing for his mid-week
Bible study when the telephone rang. Mary, his wife,
answered it. The voice she recognized easily enough. She
had heard it frequently in recent weeks. Almost every day
the same voice would ring, asking for David—sometimes
more than once in the day. This time, Mary explained that
David was not available. No, he was not out, but involved
with something else. He would ring back later.

A great sigh emitted from the other end, as though its
owner had been deeply wounded, and the line went dead.
Mary went out shopping. The phone rang again.

This time David had to leave his thought-train in full
flight. The direction of the study was just coming into focus,

and he was reluctant to leave it, but the phone call could be important.

It was 'the voice', as he had feared. For the next hour he listened again to a rigmarole with which he was now very familiar. Occasionally he was able to intersperse the flow with words of encouragement. They had been over it all before so many times! He was weary of trying to help this person see reason. The one crumb of comfort was that it was her phone bill that was running up, and not his! His train of thought for the fast-approaching Bible study had gone to the wind.

This was all part of a clergyman's life. This was what he had been called by God to do; to care for the weak and awkward, just as much as to teach those who were eager to walk closer with their Lord. As always, the Bible study that evening was a blessing to all who came expecting to find a word of help and enlightenment. David had given what time he could to its preparation. If the Lord saw fit to allow interruption, he still honoured his word.

Because a minister's home is often used for helping troubled people through their difficulties, certain pressures are brought to bear upon his family. The children, from their earliest years, are aware of broken lives frequently turning up on the doorstep, of people feeling hurt and upset, of Daddy's emergency calls away from the dinner table. They could be forgiven for deciding that Christianity is full of problems!

As a rule, little ears have very sharp hearing, and our children have to learn early in life to keep confidences, not passing on juicy little snippets of conversation overheard in Dad's study, or between him and Mother, as they share concern over a hurting soul.

Maybe, to some degree, our children do have to carry old heads on young shoulders, but there are compensations. They come in for a great deal of kindly 'spoiling', especially from elderly members of the congregation, which they soak up gladly. They have the early privilege of being part of a family whose vocation is to serve others. What a blessing it must be on their growth towards maturity, if they can learn early in life to love their neighbour in the way which Jesus taught.

Although many of the pastoral issues dealt with in the course of the ministry are concerned with problems and hang-ups of one kind or another, there are also many occasions for great joy and enrichment. We have, in our twenty-three years, been privileged to know many dear saints of God who have ministered to us in their own suffering.

Florrie was a dear lady who had been housebound for over twenty years when I first met her. Among other things, she had severely ulcerated legs which gave her an enormous amount of pain. She looked after herself and her brother, and a nurse came in regularly to dress her sores. I must have visited her dozens of times, but not once did I hear her complain about her lot. She would tell me about the pain, but it was always a statement of fact, made with a radiant smile—never a moan of dissatisfaction! Always she would share how precious the Lord Jesus had been to her on that particular day, and something that she had read in her well-worn Bible that morning. It was small wonder that on her birthday, every available shelf in her living room was smothered in cards of greeting, expressing the love of those who knew her.

Elsie is another who is in constant pain, but who just radiates the Lord's love on all who visit her. I love to sit and listen to stories of her childhood, which still live in her memory as though it were only yesterday, despite the passing of over eighty years. To take her mind off the nagging pain, she sings, 'Count Your Blessings' while washing up the dishes, and 'All Things Bright and Beautiful' when dressing! Her life is indeed a melody. She is totally in tune with her surroundings, and has learnt to bear her suffering with a song in her heart.

Dick and Lily were two of my favourite people a few years ago. They had no children of their own, but throughout their long married life, their house had been home for many. There was an atmosphere in that place which spelt peace and harmony, comfort and security. No matter what they were doing, they always had time to give to the many who dropped in on them. They were not wealthy, in terms of this world's goods, but rich beyond compare in spiritual things. Their secret, I believe, was a simple one. They prayed. Many hours they spent in prayer. Their home was steeped in prayer. Before making any decisions they always took them to the Lord. Whenever they heard of someone's distress or special need, they would spend time on their knees regularly, until the difficulty was resolved. I am sure that many, many people owe a great deal to this saintly couple's sacrifice of time, and their holy concern.

How I thank God for men and women like these, who have enriched my own life, and taught me so much of what it means to rejoice in suffering. They have shown me how to assess true values. They have, often unconsciously, made me realize the insignificance of petty little niggles which threaten to blight my walk with the Lord. We often tend to make our understanding of God and his word a complicated, puzzling business. Their faith is simple, sure, unwavering—and it works, to give them peace and contentment despite physical and emotional circumstances which might war against such serenity. They are the salt of the earth.

8

Thursdays at Three

'I'm disappointed,' said the church grouser. 'I thought you'd be a good pastor's wife, and support your husband by taking the chair at the Women's Own. Our last one did, and the one before that!'

Jane was shattered. A warm, loving person by nature, she was perfectly at home comforting and encouraging people in need, but quite terrified of a public platform or position of leadership.

Mrs Vicar is a person in her own right, with her own share of God's gifts and abilities, and they won't always stretch to every woman's idea of what she should be doing. Jane was deeply hurt by this thoughtless woman's words, and throughout her time in that place there was always a barrier between them.

Many of us do find ourselves, either willingly or out of necessity, at the front on Thursday afternoons at three, or whenever our parish Women's Fellowship or Mother's Union happens to meet. I myself escaped this privilege for the first twenty years of our life in the manse, but finally capitulated, only to discover that it is a delightfully fulfilling, meaningful role to play! Contrary to what some may think, the Women's Meeting is not the gossip corner of the church, nor does it have the air of a doctor's waiting room!

I have found stimulating fellowship, a caring community of people, whose wide interest in the Lord's work at home and overseas is remarkable. Some of our ladies even take notes while the speaker delivers his or her message, which keeps their minds on the matter in hand, and provides them with plenty to chew over at their leisure too.

Perhaps this is something that many more of us could do to our advantage during the Sunday sermon! Long ago, when my first child was a baby, and therefore my concentration during the morning service was somewhat undermined, I discovered the value of looking for just one point in the ministry that I could take home with me. It was an excellent practice at the time, but now I find that to look for just one point sometimes means that I miss the rest. What a waste of the hours my poor dear husband has put into his sermon preparation! Now, to take notes of all his main points will usually bring back the whole at a later date, and is so much more valuable to my soul.

To get back to the Women's Meeting, let us bury the myth which states that it is just for old souls who are 'past it', and who usually fall asleep in the warm atmosphere of the meeting room. Many of them are elderly, it is true, but they have a wealth of life-experience behind them, which contributes an enormous amount of wisdom and interest to the younger members of the fellowship.

It was a warm, sunny afternoon when I visited my very first Women's Meeting. I was a young college student, and was accompanying another who was an old hand at this game. She had been to at least three such meetings before, and knew exactly what to do! We had travelled the six or seven miles to this little country chapel on her motor scooter, and arrived somewhat crumpled and windswept at the door of the church hall.

'How very nice to have some young people with us today,' beamed the leader of the meeting. We were indeed very conscious of our tender years. We surveyed the assembled throng of behatted ladies, smelling of lavender and mothballs. What right had we to speak with authority to these dear souls, most of whom were old enough to be our great-grannies?

My knees were knocking and my throat felt dry. 'Don't worry,' hissed my colleague, 'they won't hear what you say; they're nearly all deaf!' That was cold comfort.

I shall never forget that day. Deaf, or not deaf, many of those ladies were alive to God, gracious, loving, caring women, willing to learn from young whippersnappers like us, anxious to include us in their prayers.

'Thank you, my dear,' one crippled lady said to me afterwards, as she reached out a bony hand from her wheelchair. 'You've done me good! I could see you were nervous, and so I put you in our dear Lord's hands, and he put his words in your mouth. God bless you, dear child.' It was a benediction on my young and inexperienced head.

In the group where I am presently privileged to be a little involved, we follow a regular plan of teaching, interspersed with visits from missionaries, or Bible College students about to embark on their life-ministry. The year's programme is sprinkled with a number of special events, including a couple of do-it-yourself afternoons, when the members themselves contribute thoughts and share how the Lord has recently been helping them. With our oldest member having just celebrated her ninety-eighth birthday, and quite a few more closely following on her heels, we have lively, enjoyable times together.

Of course, the annual outing to the seaside has to be observed, as it has been happening since the year 'dot'. It seems to be a time for reminiscing together over past outings: the days when they chartered a charabanc, and drove in style, though not with much comfort; the year that Gladys lost her teeth in the mud at Southend; the time when it rained all day, and they had to go home early. Alas, they are not all happy memories!

This past year we took two of them in wheelchairs, and the chief quest of the day was finding suitable toilets for them both! Always there have been a few spare seats on the coach for one or two friends and neighbours, and we see this event as quite a specialized form of outreach, an opportunity to introduce other women to a Christian fellowship.

Recently I was looking through the minutes book from the committee meetings. The notes went back to the years when I was in my cradle. It was thrilling to read of frequent reports of women coming to know Jesus as their Saviour during those years—and they still do!

Bertha had been coming to us on a Thursday afternoon for about a year, brought originally by a friend from the Over-Sixties Club. One week one of our church members, who was himself about to enter the Christian ministry, came to talk to the ladies about the errors of Jehovah's Witness teaching, and how to handle them on the doorstep. Having once been an active member of that sect, he was well equipped to speak on the subject. Unbeknown to us, Bertha's son was a Jehovah's Witness, and she was very perturbed by some of the things which were pointed out that afternoon. Later the same day she handed her own life over to the Lord, and some months afterwards, despite her seventy-eight years and an inherent fear of water, she was baptized by immersion, signifying her commitment to the Lord Jesus. Today she rejoices in knowing him as her own personal Saviour, and readily shares with her family and friends the reality of her Christian faith.

Myrtle was a younger woman, living in a small village a few miles out of town. A near neighbour of hers was having an extension built onto her house. 'We're increasing our family,' she explained to Myrtle, 'from the other end! It's going to be a granny flat for my mum-in-law. Since John's dad died, she doesn't like being alone.'

When eventually Mum-in-law arrived, she found that her problem of loneliness was not much relieved! The family were rarely at home. Most of the villagers seemed immersed in their own lives, and showed no interest in her. Myrtle, however, was different. She had always enjoyed people's company, no matter who they were, and took to calling on Mrs Dunn two or three times a week. She soon learnt that the old lady had been an active worker in the Salvation Army for most of her life, and was now missing the fellowship very much indeed. Myrtle knew nothing about church or religion, and was not much good on the tambourine, but offered to take her to a meeting once a week if she would like.

Apparently the Salvation Army did not have a meeting place anywhere near, but a few miles away, in the nearest town, there was a Women's Meeting held in a Baptist church on Thursday afternoons. So it was that Mrs Dunn and Myrtle started to come to our Women's Christian Fellowship. To the old lady it was 'home from home', and became a weekly delight. To Myrtle it was something totally new in her experience.

The first day she felt a bit like a fish out of water, but was greatly warmed by the welcome she received from the other women there. She found that she was looking forward to taking her friend each week, and later, when Mrs Dunn was unwell, she quite happily went alone. Gradually she grew into a personal faith in the Lord Jesus, and was grateful that her neighbour's mother had come to live in her village. As she said herself: 'It was her coming to live near us that put me in the way of hearing the Good News!'

The other important factor leading up to Myrtle's conversion was undoubtedly the warmth of Christian fellowship that she found in that Women's Meeting. I am convinced that if we are to evangelize, we must befriend. If somebody comes to our church, our Women's Meeting, or even our home, and finds the atmosphere chilly, people huddled together in cosy little cliques, they are most unlikely to come again.

I have always been interested in flowers, and once attended a meeting of a Floral Art Society in the town where we lived at the time. They took my money at the door. I watched the demonstration. I stayed for a full half-hour afterwards. Not a soul spoke to me. Three times I attempted the beginnings of a conversation, but was completely ignored. I never went again.

God forbid that people coming into our churches should ever be frozen out like this. If we would win them, we must also woo them. Myrtle is one of many, whose initial interest in the gospel grew because it was wrapped in love. She felt herself to be part of the group long before she really was. She knew she was wanted.

If it is important that our Women's Meetings provide a comfortable atmosphere for newcomers, it is equally important that the content of the meetings appeals to their needs. I am a great believer in the scriptural and natural principle of sowing the seed, feeding and watering it, allowing God's life-giving power to fill it, and then reaping the harvest. In a meeting where people are regularly in attendance, we have time to let the seed grow. A structured programme, leading up to the occasional overtly evangelistic meeting will provide the right climate to reap a spiritual harvest. In no way does this limit the Lord's regenerating power to these 'come-to-Jesus-meetings', but it does provide a particular opportunity for women to nail their colours to the mast, and make their decision clear.

Is it possible to aim at two targets, and hit them both? I think so. Especially if they are both situated in line with one another. Spare a few minutes to watch an accomplished snooker player, and you will see what I mean.

Our first aim, in the Women's Meeting, is to introduce people to their Saviour. The second is to provide the right environment for developing their faith, and sharing fellowship with one another.

A number of women do the rounds of these specialized

meetings, yet rarely go to church on Sundays. Tuesday afternoon is when the Methodists hold their 'Bright Hour' for women; on Wednesday the Anglican Coffee Morning Fellowship meets, and later the Sisterhood at the Brethren Chapel; and still they come to us on Thursday afternoons. Their Christian teaching comes entirely from these afternoon gatherings, and, while we encourage them to share fellowship with other members of the family of God, a little careful thought and planning can produce a programme of biblical instruction that will help them to understand the gospel and grow in the Christian faith.

Many speakers delight in being given a subject, especially when they know that it is fitting in with an overall theme. Here are a few suggestions of the sort of subjects that might help a Women's Meeting to become a seat of learning, as well as a happy fellowship experience:

How to know my prayers are heard
How to enjoy my Bible
How to cope with loneliness
     —or depression
     —or bereavement
Can the Bible be trusted?
Is God really three people?
What the resurrection means to me

Perhaps a short series on Bible characters such as:

Women of the Old Testament (Hannah, Ruth, Miriam, Esther, etc)
Men of the New Testament (Thomas, Stephen, Barnabas, etc)

The less there is said about them in the Bible, the more compact and punchy a study of such characters can become! You would need at least three weeks for Abraham, Moses or David.

Variety is indeed the spice of life! Intersperse these

programmed talks with those by a missionary home on furlough, or a friend invited to share some way in which the Lord has been blessing her recently. Ask some of the local clergy to come and address the group occasionally. This helps to foster good relationships with the other churches, and if, as is possible, you have one or two of his own 'flock' in attendance at your meeting, it is a special joy for them to have their own vicar or minister there too.

Those good relationships can be spoilt, however, not just where visiting clergy are concerned, but with any guest speaker, when the matter of expenses is raised, or not raised, as the case may be!

'How much was your bus fare?' I was once asked at the close of a meeting where I had been speaking.

'I came by car,' I replied.

'Oh, that's all right then,' the lady said, and pocketed the meagre coins she had hoped might cover my bus fare!

Another time, having travelled several miles by bus to conduct a church anniversary, my husband and I were brought home in the church leader's car, as the bus service did not coincide with the timing of the meeting. We were not reimbursed for the outward journey; my husband was given no fee for his services; and, to crown it all, on dropping us outside our home, the car driver asked if we could help towards the petrol! Sadly, whenever I think of that church or the person involved, this incident always comes to mind, and clouds my thoughts concerning that place.

Apart from anything else, surely it is good manners to give an expression of thanks to one who has given time and effort to minister at your meeting. Some Women's Meetings are notoriously mean! A fifty pence piece, to cover ten miles of travel and many hours put into preparation of the ministry is hardly adequate. It is acutely embarrassing to be offered expenses by an anxious looking treasurer, who quite obviously hopes you will decline. Calculate the visitor's expenses carefully, I would say generously, seal them in an envelope addressed with her name, and hand it over without any fuss or bother. Both of you will be spared anxious moments. When the Lord Jesus sent out some of his people to spread the gospel, (as recorded in Luke 10) he told them to accept expenses, for 'a labourer is worthy of his hire'.

If a meeting is small and funds inadequate, perhaps the leader and committee of that meeting need to reassess their commitment to it. It might be necessary to readjust the giving of their personal tithe to the Lord, so that this part of his work does not go wanting. I have sometimes been surprised by the generosity of the small groups and the stinginess of the big ones!

This whole matter of making the visiting speaker feel comfortable contributes to the general effect of the meeting. Sometimes one is left to sit in splendid isolation out front, while the leader busies herself with a number of last-minute details which should have been thought out long before she got there.

I once arrived at a neighbouring church, having been booked some months previously. I was not reminded of the meeting nearer the date, so felt a slight apprehension as to whether I was expected. The place was in semi-darkness, but to my surprise there were already some ladies sitting inside, apparently enjoying the gloom. One was busying herself with the kettle and appeared to be in charge.

'I think I am due to be here today,' I began.

'Oh yes, that's right, dearie. Mrs Jones told me you were coming. She won't be here today, so she said you could lead the meeting—all right? Oh, we haven't a pianist. She usually plays too, you see. So perhaps you could do it, or if not, just choose a hymn we all know.'

'Well, all right,' I said, trying to take it all in my stride. 'Do you think we could have some light?'

'If you think we really need it. Perhaps just one. We're

trying to save electricity, you see.'

One thing I *couldn't* do too well was see! At the end of the meeting I suggested that perhaps somebody might have some notices to give. Nobody rose to the idea immediately, but then my kettle-lady said that she thought the meeting might be closing for good at the end of the month, so they had better all come the following week to find out! I was not altogether surprised.

In all fairness, I think there are only a few Women's Meetings that are run in this haphazard fashion. Most leaders give careful time and thought to the structure of each week's session. For the most part, it is prudent to keep the format of each one very much the same. Most women feel comfortable and 'safe' in familiar surroundings. If they have always had a hymn and prayer to begin with, the notices half way through, and a cup of tea at the end, they are probably much happier if it is kept that way. While variety of subject matter can keep a group of people exercising a lively interest, too many innovations can kill their appreciation of all you are trying to do.

Since you know the subject which your speaker is going to expound, you are one up when it comes to planning the other items to fit into the hour. Hymns and choruses will, of course, support the theme. Some of the prayer-time will be directly related to the topic for the day. The hour spent there will come together as a whole, and while some of the details of what is said will escape some people's memory, they will have imbibed the general message much more readily than when the meeting is made up of a number of disjointed items.

One of the things that I have learned during our years in the leadership of a church is that it is often much easier to get on with a job myself than to delegate. People don't always run at my own pace; their ideas don't always match up with mine; sometimes they are unreliable or fractious.

Easier it may be to DIY, but it is definitely not the right

way to lead! Nobody will develop a strong character if they have been constantly restrained and never allowed to express their point of view. We are into the business of building disciples of God. If they are to develop a vital Christian faith and character, they must be allowed to work out that faith in their own way. When women in the meeting are given the opportunity to contribute, by leading in prayer, sharing a personal blessing, reading the scriptures, giving out books or being responsible for the tea, they will feel themselves to be involved. It is so much more fulfilling to be part of the organization, rather than a mere observer. So include them in the weekly running of the meeting. Perhaps, when the Bible is read, and you have overcome the 'which version' problem in your church, it could be read in unison. This way, even the shy members have a chance to hear their own voices. There must be a multitude of ways in which we can involve people to a point where they feel that they are necessary, appreciated members of the fellowship. We must exploit these ways if we want our group to flourish.

Another reason why it must be very wrong to think that it is better to do the job myself, is the motive which prompts that thought. Presumably I think myself more capable than anyone else. Apart from the obvious sin of pride, this is also a very wrong conclusion to draw! God has equipped me, it is true, to do what he wants me to do, but I am also very fallible, as my Women's Fellowship know only too well.

Some months ago my mother was staying with us and came with me to the Thursday afternoon meeting.

'I didn't know you had a mother,' one dear lady remarked, wide-eyed. We smiled. I wanted to say, 'Did you think I just fell out of heaven, then?' But I knew she didn't think that, and neither did any of the others. I seem to be frequently forgetting things they have asked me to announce, calling people by the wrong names, and generally making many mistakes. We laugh about it together, and sometimes they even make excuses for me when I have dropped yet another clanger. They know I am far from being the perfect Women's Meeting leader, and I know it too. We understand each other, and that goes a long way towards a happy, growing relationship.

9

Clergy Are People Too

It was a hot, sultry evening in June. The church was crowded to the point of discomfort, and I wished fervently that we had not come. It was the start of our annual holiday, and we could have been wandering over the cliffs, watching the sun sink slowly into the sea, instead of sitting here, squashed in between a large, behatted, perspiring lady and a young man, whose choice of aftershave somewhat offended my nose—or was it the wilting lady?

So crowded was this popular preaching centre, that we couldn't even sit together, which was a pity, because the ministry so exactly fitted our situation at that time, and I needed my husband's hand to squeeze!

Perhaps it was the word of God that was really getting to me, and not the aftershave, or the wilting lady, or the desire for the big outdoors.

'Abraham was wrong,' declared the preacher. 'He desperately wanted a son, so he ran ahead of God and took Hagar—and the fruit of that union, the Arab race, has been at variance with Israel from that day to this!'

This was not what I wanted to hear. We weren't running ahead of God! Like Abraham I too longed for a son, a baby to cuddle, someone to care for, whose life I could have a share in shaping. Only two days before coming away we had sent off applications to an adoption society. Some people had told us that childlessness was quite common among the clergy and the medical profession, people who live with certain emotional pressures.

Be that as it may, it had become a source of very real distress. Of course we had prayed about it a good deal, and felt it right to take this step, but now this wretched preacher had destroyed my peace of mind about it all, and my dreams of little woolly coats and bonnets would have to be buried again.

I didn't sing the last hymn. Something seemed to cloud my eyes so I couldn't read the words. We stepped out into the sunshine, but it didn't feel warm and bright any longer. We drove back to the borrowed caravan in silence, both knowing that the Lord had spoken to us, not liking what he had said. Usually I found the Lord's word uplifting and encouraging, but this night I really felt he had delivered a blow below the belt, especially after leading us on to apply for a baby!

In my naïve way I had fondly imagined that within a couple of months or so there would be a little 'bundle of joy' disturbing our nights and filling our washing line with nappies, and I would love every minute of it. But now, what had I to look forward to? I felt bitter towards the Lord, angry that he had let us be in that particular church at that particular time.

'Darling, I think you missed the promise!'

'What promise?' I retorted. 'He hasn't kept his promise. He's taken it away!'

'Isaac, of course! God promised to give Abraham his very own child, Isaac. I feel that the Lord told us tonight that he will give us a child of our own. Isn't that something great!'

Suddenly the rising rage within me melted. Trust Eddie to get it right! Inside my head I was shouting so loudly in protest at what I thought the Lord was depriving me of, that

I had completely missed the promise. I had missed his best!

That summer holiday was one of the best we have ever had. The sun shone constantly and we revelled in the beauties of moor and seascape. One morning we rose with the sun, and ran up the hill in our nightclothes to watch a colony of rabbits hold their early morning council. We grew closer to our dear Lord and to each other, and the 'sadness' that had been with us since the early days of our marriage seemed to take on different proportions altogether. The end was in sight. Had not God said so? He would meet our need, as he always does.

On our return from holiday a pile of letters lay scattered across the doormat, among them a long, slim envelope from the Adoption Society. I was not eager to open it. What if they were offering us a baby already? In the light of what had happened that would be a hard test, and I was not sure that I could easily let the opportunity pass. I guess our loving Lord knew my weakness at this point; at any rate he didn't put me to the test. The short but friendly letter gently suggested that we postpone our application for at least two years; and I was relieved!

Very quickly life returned to its normal, hectic pattern. The doors of our home were frequently being opened to broken people needing support. There were meetings to lead, 'shut-ins' to visit, a Sunday School to organize, and a hundred and one other things to keep me busy. Certainly I didn't sit around moping and waiting for the miracle to happen.

One day, at a low emotional ebb, one of our young wives nearly threw me completely:

'I suppose you don't want to have any children, do you Cynthia?' she said. 'You wouldn't be able to do all your work in the church if there was a family to look after, would you?'

Now, that was a very sore spot! As if it was not bad enough having to lead the Young Wives' group, listening to all their baby-chatter and still keep smiling! Now, here was one of them, no doubt a spokeswoman for the rest, calmly assuming that we had actually chosen to be childless!

Sometimes, through the years, I wondered if we had completely misunderstood the Lord's voice on that sultry Sunday evening in June, but always at such times, words of comfort and assurance would seem to jump out from the page as I read my Bible daily. Our God is not a hard taskmaster; he leads gently, cushioning every blow to our faith. Surely without disappointments and trials we would be spineless creatures, spiritual jellyfish!

The Young Wives' group continued to be a little thorn in my side, mainly, I suppose, because it made me so aware of what I was not—a mum. One morning, amid much laughter and chatter, we were preparing the church hall for their annual party. Elizabeth and I began to hump a piano into a more suitable position. It was heavy.

'It's a good job you're not pregnant,' she laughed. I stood stock still. She must have read my face very well indeed, for then she burst out:

'You're not, are you?'

And I was. Only that morning my doctor had confirmed it. And so it was, that almost seven years from the day of the Lord's special promise to us, our son, Jonathan, was born. I wish I could say that throughout those waiting years I had implicit, unflinching trust that he would keep his promise! I only know that he is faithful, and so gracious, for two years later Jonathan's little sister arrived to make our family complete.

As with any young couple starting a family, our lives changed considerably when the babies finally came. It was, perhaps, more noticeable for us, because for many years we had functioned in a very close partnership, totally committed to the requirements of our church fellowship. Probably the most significant adjustment that I had to make, as the minister's wife, was to be much less involved in the life of the church.

At first, although I must whisper it very quietly, it was quite a welcome change, but as time went by I began to feel quite on the fringe of things, and I didn't like it. I began to wonder if Christian fellowship meant more to me than time spent alone with my Lord! Heaven forbid that a clergy wife should be guilty of such spiritual slackness!

When Mary's family arrived, she too dropped out of her responsibilities in the Sunday School and the women's work. Her weekly trip to church on Sunday morning was usually fraught with tantrums from the twins, so that, before very long, she didn't even try to go to worship. Her reaction was quite different from mine, but equally harmful.

She found that she no longer looked for Christian fellowship of any kind. She was quite content to leave the running of church matters to her husband, and to construct her own little world around herself and her babies. In time this began to eat away at her marriage. What a blessing that she and her husband saw what was coming, and prayerfully sought to rebuild the crumbling pieces before they fell into complete disarray.

I believe that front-liners come in for a particular kind of spiritual attack. Ministers, vicars, missionaries and their families are people too! They are just as vulnerable as any of their parishioners, just as human, just as fallible. Some may think them impervious to temptation, or at least to yielding to it, but unhappily the high expectation of others often brings extra pressure upon the already harassed parson and his wife.

If the attack is of a spiritual nature, so ought the counter-attack to be. In his letter to the believers in Ephesus, Paul gives us a marvellous picture of the Christian soldier kitted out, ready for battle. Each piece of armour is described in detail, and over it all is carried the shield of faith. Wearing our spiritual chainmail we are well equipped to face our spiritual warfare, for we are assured that the shield of faith will 'quench all the flaming darts of the evil one' (Eph 6:6).

It has often been pointed out that this description of God-given armour provides no protection for the back of the body, reminding us that we must meet our Enemy face-on.

It also speaks to me of our need for back-up support, particularly when we are in the front line of spiritual battle. Your minister and his family need your support, not your criticism. If his preaching or some action or misdeed of his upsets you, don't tell him he is no good, or worse still share your opinions with someone else; encourage him to do better!

A certain church just south of London was considering the appointment of a new pastor. A members' meeting was called to assess the suitability of a prospective candidate. One man, whose authority within the fellowship was well respected, let it be known that he was personally against the appointment, but he very graciously added: 'If the rest of the meeting want to go ahead, I promise to give my total support to this man.' They did go ahead; and he kept his promise, and was greatly blessed in doing so.

'We pray for you and your family every Friday,' she said. 'It would be so much better if we could know specific items for prayer.' So, on the first Sunday in every month I give her a written list of items for praise and petition. During the last eighteen months that dear lady and her husband have helped us through a number of family crises, extra responsibilities and difficult decisions. We can never overestimate the power of prayer, and a congregation's prayer support is essential to the spiritual vitality of its leader.

David's father died just before Christmas one year. He conducted the funeral himself. There followed a week of hectic activity in his church, and all the time, as the leader of the festivities, he appeared to be merry and bright. Only his wife knew how deeply he felt the pain of this sudden shock. Never before had she seen her husband cry, night after night, sobbing into his pillow.

Over the years David had been a source of strength and comfort to many families in their hour of need, but nobody came to help him in his own bereavement. Perhaps his parishioners had forgotten that he too was a mere man and needed the human touch just as much as anyone else. The nightly outbursts were his salvation. They released the tension which no doubt was increased by his efforts to continue pastoring his flock at this time. Two of the families within his congregation were surrounded with very deep problems, and David was frequently called in to be the support they expected from their minister.

It was a hard winter for him and his wife, but they learnt some precious lessons from the Lord. The end of the apostle Paul's second letter to young Timothy became especially meaningful: 'All deserted me.... But the Lord stood by me and gave me strength to proclaim the word fully.... The Lord will rescue me from every evil and save me for his heavenly kingdom' (2 Tim 4:16–18). This time their church fellowship had failed them, but their Lord and Saviour never would.

I suppose that we all have patches in our lives when it seems as though the sun will never shine again. Often these prove to be not only the test-beds of our faith, but also the growing periods, where our Christian character and trust in God is concerned. When a member of the church congregation finds himself enveloped in such difficulties, he will frequently seek out his pastor for support and possibly for advice, but where does that pastor go when he himself is facing indecision and perplexing circumstances? Unless he has a supportive fellowship around him, he and his wife will find themselves at the end of the line, with no one else to turn to on the human level.

Rachel was a 'mish-kid'. At fifteen she was beginning to kick over the traces. If only she could spread her wings and

fly away to where life was really happening! But a girls'
boarding school, situated miles from anywhere, hardly gave
scope for such frivolity.

The first few years of her life had been spent in a far-off
land, where Mum and Dad were translating the Bible for
some backward tribe of people. She had known nothing
else during those years, and had been perfectly content to
play with little brown children, who hardly ever wore
clothes, and to learn her lessons on Mothers' knee. When
she was seven, it was deemed necessary to send her to a
school for missionaries' children, hundreds of miles away
from home. She had enjoyed that too, had made some
close friends and had lots of fun. But even then there had
been a lot of emotional ups and downs for one so tender in
years. The first two nights of term were always tearful. Her
mother's brave smile and forced cheerfulness never failed
to leave Rachel wishing she didn't have to be left behind at
school. And again, at the end of each term, to have to part
with one's dearest and closest friends for a whole six weeks
seemed unbearable!

Now, here she was in England, which she could never
think of as 'home', cooped up in this dreadful school with
thousands of rules to keep, and loads of work to do. Mum
and Dad had left her behind yet again; now, of course, for
much longer than it used to be, and she was learning that
there were endless possibilities of fun and experience out
there in the big, wide world, if only one could shake off the
restraint of school and all its rules. No girl was allowed out
on her own, and never without permission. Weekends were
spent in study, organized activity and church. There was no
freedom, none at all, and Rachel wanted desperately to
escape.

Within a year Mum and Dad had returned from the
Mission Field, anxious to protect their daughter from all
that seemed to be pulling her away from the straight and
narrow. Was it too late? Had they been wrong in spending

their lives devoted to the Lord's special service, possibly at the expense of their own daughter's well-being? How could they make up the ground they appeared to have lost?

Dad was an ordained Anglican clergyman, and was offered a country parish for the duration of their stay in England. So it was that a small congregation in Kent found themselves with a new vicar who was somewhat unfamiliar with the way of life in this country, having been out of it for sixteen years, and who also had a giant-sized personal anxiety to carry.

'Bear one another's burdens, and so fulfil the law of Christ,' so ran the message, taken from Galatians 6:2, and preached at his Institution in that place. The parishioners rose to the challenge. They were used to bearing each other's burdens. Such is sometimes the way of village life. Now they were willing, indeed anxious, to take the heavy weight from the shoulders of their new vicar and his wife.

Three of the women belonged to a Prayer Circle, which met together once a fortnight, but was committed to pray every day for certain issues. The vicarage family was immediately put on the list for prayer.

When Rachel came home, to her parents' great joy, she quickly became friends with another girl of her own age who was a keen young Christian.

The first winter was an exceptionally cold one, and after many years in the tropics, the vicar and his wife were easy prey for all the coughs, colds and sneezes that were going about. Always there was somebody ready to do the shopping or whatever was necessary, even to stand in at a parish meeting or on Sundays.

It was a long, dark winter for them both before Rachel really came through her growing pains. In fact it lasted some years! But through it all that little congregation of the Lord's people held up its leaders constantly in prayer, and poured in its support and love to an extraordinary degree. Needless to say, the fellowship grew. God honoured their practical faith and showered them with blessings. As they willingly gave of themselves, so he taught them and encouraged them to go further and to obtain precious promises.

Perhaps what I am trying to say is this: the Christian church is a family. In a human family there are mums and dads and grandparents and children and aunts and uncles and cousins. They all have different personalities, though certain family traits; they are all at different stages of physical and emotional development; they all have varying experiences. They each have their own individual rights; sometimes they disagree with one another. If one member of the family is hurting, the rest will be affected by it— hopefully by showing concern and giving support. I know that not all families are supportive; not all behave as an ideal family should. Just because that is a fact, does it have to be accepted?

The power of the Lord Jesus Christ is known to be dynamic. His influence within a life can drastically change that person's attitude as well as his lifestyle. We are talking about the Christian church, the family of God. Surely, if Jesus is given his rightful place in the family, he will then be allowed to exert his influence on those people to create a loving, caring environment for every man, woman and child within the fellowship.

I am a mother, and to some extent my home and the people in it revolve around me. But I am no more important, no more valid as a person, than my youngest child. I do for her certain things that she is unable to cope with herself, but she, in turn and quite unconsciously most of the time, gives to me a sense of being needed, a purpose for much of my activity, a share in a loving relationship. We laugh together, and have been known to cry together. I scold her when necessary. Sometimes she has to put me right too! Am I too proud to accept rebuke from my own offspring, when it is called for? I hope not.

In a family the size of many of our local churches, it is of course necessary to have leaders; men and women who have been called and equipped by God to serve his family in that particular way. Their task is to teach the word and to lead their people into a deeper relationship with him. Until recent years it would seem that more and more responsibility has been laid at the feet of the 'professional' Christian leader. Happily we are now waking up to the scriptural principle of recognizing spiritual gifts in the laity, and learning to share the workload. However the sheer volume of pastoral care needed in any local community, and the high standard of Bible teaching required, still demands that there be leaders appointed. Those leaders will blossom and flourish, only as they are nurtured by the people among whom they work. The family feeling must be strong. Don't leave your vicar to cope with his dark days alone. 'Bear one another's burdens, and so fulfil the law of Christ' (Gal 6:2).

IO

Left Holding the Baby

'At last, B-Day! Jonathan Craig was born at 5:17 pm, a funny, wrinkled little thing, but maybe he'll one day be better looking, like his dad. It still seems rather like a dream; I can hardly believe it has happened to me!'

So runs the entry in my diary for May 26th 1971. What a day of rejoicing it was in our family, after all the waiting.

Jesus reminds us, in Luke 15:7, that there is great joy in heaven over one sinner that repents. The moment of spiritual birth is a joy to behold from the heavenly viewpoint, and likewise on earth. Many witnessing Christians have the privilege of acting as spiritual midwives, and somehow, in that moment, all the agonies of the emotional or mental struggle which may have preceded it, just pale into insignificance. Though the labour pains may be excruciating, they are always forgotten when the babe emerges. In the gospel of John, Jesus himself described this supernatural happening in a man's life as being 'born again'. Peter, speaking to new Christians, referred to them as 'newborn babes' (1 Pet 2:2). It seems to be the most apt way of describing a person's position when they confess their sinfulness before God, and accept all that the Lord Jesus Christ has done on their behalf.

Leaders within a thriving church family will find themselves frequently left holding the baby. In this chapter we are going to look into some of the ways in which we can help these new Christians to find their feet, and begin to grow up into spiritual maturity.

If you were to spend a day in a hospital nursery, you would quickly discover that all babies differ from one another. Some are comatose, some hyperactive, some seem to be always yelling, some are totally contented. They each have a personality of their own, and new Christians tend to be the same! They are not all turned out of the same 'evangelimould', thank goodness. They all have individual needs, and therefore require careful attention within the church family.

If a baby is to grow up to be a happy, responsible, co-ordinated person, he must have love. It is not always easy. Sometimes he is smelly, often very demanding, but a mother's heart responds to his every need. He needs his cuddle-times, a physical contact with his mother; and our 'new babes in Christ' need us. In an atmosphere of loving fellowship, where they feel at ease to air their queries and talk about all that is happening in their lives, they will grow naturally, at their own pace. I have been fascinated to see how some seem to mature in great leaps and bounds, while others slowly, steadily develop a deep, unshakeable faith.

'Like newborn babes, long for the pure spiritual milk,' said the apostle Peter to his new protégés in the faith. Without the nourishment of milk a baby will die. Right from the word 'go' our young Christians must be encouraged to read the word of God. To many, the Bible is an unknown book. It is no use telling them that they ought to read it. We must show them how to do so, with understanding. Being a Christian is not keeping a set of rules; rather it is building a relationship. If a young believer, or an older one for that matter, breaks the rules one morning and fails to have his quiet time, does that mean that everything will go badly for him that day? I'm sure that some Christians tend to regard their daily Bible reading and prayer time as a kind of fetish that must be observed at all costs, lest some nasty accident befall them! Don't let us ever give the impression that keeping a daily tryst with God is one of the rules we ought to keep. Things that we 'ought' to do usually carry the implication that we don't want to do them, but must do all the same! It is, of course, an excellent habit to form, and essential to one's spiritual growth and health, but if we put the emphasis on getting to know Jesus, and manage to convey the thrill of learning from the living word of God, our babes will develop their own appetite for spiritual food.

The evening of June 23rd 1984 was cold and wet. Jane and Stuart remember it well, because it turned out to be their birthday! For several weeks they had frequently seen big posters proclaiming that an Argentinian evangelist had arrived with a special message for London. He would be preaching nightly in one of London's major football arenas. Neither Jane nor Stuart were particularly interested in this 'special message', but it would be a free evening's entertainment, so they went along for a bit of a giggle.

Sitting high up in the stands surrounding the football pitch, they peered down at the evangelist and his entourage—all of whom seemed very remote, just matchstick men away in the distance. The seats were hard, and a cold draught whistled round their ankles. Jane shivered. Somewhere near by a baby persistently cried. Why ever didn't the mother take it away? Perhaps she, like them, was stuck in the middle of a row, and just couldn't get by without treading on everybody's toes.

There was a lot of singing, unfamiliar songs, but the band was good. Stuart thought they were quite professional. He appreciated good strong music, but was surprised that everyone sang so lustily. He looked around him. Most of the people looked as though they were enjoying it. Funny that! To him, music was something to listen to. Only singers actually sang!

On the programme which they had been given on arrival, there was announced a surprise guest from the sporting world. Jane was surprised, and delighted, when it turned out to be a tall young tennis player from Nigeria, currently playing in the Wimbledon tournament. She was an ardent tennis fan, and this was an unexpected pleasure. He stood, tall and smiling, and told of how the Lord Jesus Christ had given him a purpose in life. He was hoping to do well at Wimbledon, he said, but if he was knocked out it wouldn't be the end of the world! Jesus was his first love, not tennis, and he found his Christian faith meaningful and stimulating.

By now the atmosphere seemed a little warmer, the baby had stopped crying, and Jane and Stuart were beginning to feel part of this vast crowd. Then it began to rain. The evangelist took his stand. He apparently had a lot to say. They listened. When he had finished preaching, he invited people to step out and identify themselves with the Lord Jesus Christ, to hand their lives over to him, confessing their sinfulness and accepting his sacrifice on their behalf. Jane didn't altogether understand it, but she knew she must go! She stole a sidelong glance at Stuart. He seemed to be lost in thought. She gently nudged him, hoping he would let her by, but instead he joined her as she stumbled along the row of other people's legs and down the steps to the turf. They stood in the pouring rain, and there they were born again!

Before the week was out, they had been visited by a local minister, invited to a church in their locality and also to a small discussion group in somebody's house.

The last time they had been to church was for their wedding! They were a little apprehensive, but it was a good experience. The discussion group was something that really counted for them during the next few weeks. Each Friday they met with seven others, most of whom, like themselves, were brand new Christians.

On the first occasion, the minister who had previously

visited them took them in his car and introduced them to the group. They were warmly welcomed. The music coming out of the stereo unit in the corner of the room sounded vaguely familiar. Why yes, it was a song the great crowd in the football stadium had sung the other night! Stuart liked it. It helped him to voice his feelings of joy and worship to the Lord Jesus. He found himself quietly singing along with the record, and some of the others joined in too.

When the music stopped, the leader suggested that they all introduce themselves to each other, each person spending one whole minute talking about themselves to another whom they had not previously met. Then the position was reversed; and afterwards they took turns at introducing their new friend to the group. They very quickly felt that they belonged together, and time would tell that many lasting relationships were begun that evening.

A pile of Good News Bibles were placed on the coffee table, and the leader explained that this was so that they would all be using the same version, and could refer to the various parts of the Bible by page numbers. Jane and Stuart didn't know that there was more than one version of the Bible, and were most surprised to see how readable and up-to-date the language and illustrations were.

'We'll turn to page 113 in the New Testament,' said the leader, 'where we find Luke chapter 23. Would somebody please read the first paragraph.'

The study session progressed very simply, with different people taking turns at reading aloud and offering comments or asking questions. Nobody was forced to contribute, but they all felt comfortable and so it was quite natural that each have his or her say.

The new Christian 'babes' were taking their milk. In a few weeks they would be gradually weaned on to 'solids'. Some of the hard lumps would need some help in digesting. They would be learning to feed themselves, keeping a regular time of communion with their Lord each day. They would discover that there is much more to the Christian life than being born again, and would be reaching out for more teaching and experience, becoming more independent, yet enjoying and benefiting from regular fellowship with other Christians.

'Now we have five minutes in hand,' said the Bible study leader, when they had finished looking at Luke 23. 'We'll spend the time in prayer. I'd like you each to take part.' Jane gulped. This could be embarrassing.

'We'll turn to Psalm 138, near the middle of your Bibles. Read it quietly to yourselves, then select one thing from that psalm which you are personally thankful for, and turn it into a one-sentence prayer. When you are all ready, we'll bow our heads and give thanks to God.'

It wasn't so bad! When Jane had read the short psalm, she had found several things that she was really happy about, and was only too glad to voice her feelings to God in the hearing of her new friends.

These 'nursery groups' lasted for six weeks, during which Jane and Stuart became familiar with the basics of the Christian faith. They discovered how to enjoy the Bible, which until then had been only a textbook, and a rather dry one at that! They learnt to express their worship towards the Lord, and also how to pray for themselves and others. Sharing positively answered prayer each week was a thrill! Learning that prayer is not always answered as we would wish was not quite so easy to assimilate, but through it all they were beginning to discover what it means to know God, and to live in fellowship with him, always accepting that his will is best.

In a church where men and women and young people are constantly being added to the ranks of believers, it is most helpful to hold such a 'nursery group', or discipleship course, or whatever you like to call it, at periodic intervals. If you feel that it is called for in your local fellowship, perhaps the following summary will help to clarify the

major points in this programme:
1. Getting people to the group:
   a) Invite.
   b) Remind.
   c) Arrange to meet and escort to the meeting place.
2. Make them comfortable:
   a) Introduce newcomers, and get them talking together.
3. Avoid embarrassing anyone.
4. Bible study:
   a) Keep it simple.
   b) Make it enjoyable.
   c) Provide a modern version (same edition if possible, so as to find the place using page numbers, not Bible books as these will be unfamiliar).
   d) Choose suitable passages, preferably in a gospel.
   e) Frequently refer to other parts of scripture using questions such as: 'Is there anything else in the Bible which supports this idea?' or: 'Turn to page 65. [And giving the Bible reference] What does this say about the subject we are thinking of?'
   f) Draw people into discussion, using such questions as: 'Has anyone here experienced this?' or: 'How does this relate to our lives today?'
   g) At the first session, ask for volunteers to read. Some people hate doing it!
   h) Show how to look things up in the Bible, using margins, finding places, etc.
   i) Watch your language! Write down simple definitions of spiritually technical words.
5. Encourage new Christians to express their faith by asking leading questions about their first impressions, what helped them to take the step towards God and such like. It is useful to ask questions that begin with the letter 'w': why, when, what, where? These questions usually require more than 'yes' or 'no' in reply, and help the person to define their thoughts.

6. Group prayer:
   a) Put this towards end of meeting, when people are more relaxed and have already heard their own voices.
   b) Keep it short. Five minutes is sufficient, to start with.
   c) Suggest a few moments of silent prayer.
   d) Give headings, e.g. praise, thanks, family, work, selves.
   e) Give time to list, or write a one-sentence prayer.
   f) Read a psalm or hymn together, and each select a thought to turn into prayer.
   g) Limit each contribution to just one or two sentences.
7. Introduce the idea of worship as expressed in song— either a simple chorus, or use a track from a record or cassette.
8. Fellowship does not mean 'bath buns and choruses', but a cup of coffee at the end of this type of meeting does wonders for loosening the vocal cords if they are still a bit tight!

There is indeed great joy over every spiritual birth. I think that perhaps there is even greater joy felt as we see those 'babes in Christ' grow up into strong, witnessing Christians, exhibiting the Lord's power in their lives.

Unfortunately, though, not all who show great promise at the start go on to develop a healthy mind and sound limbs. We can do much to encourage when the early enthusiasm is fading, and we have to face the fact that we do have an Enemy; that doubts concerning faith are quite normal; that being a Christian can be very tough going. But after all is said and done, each person still has a free will to choose whether or not they go on with the Lord. In Matthew 13, it says that some of the seed fell along the footpath; some on rocky ground; some among thistles. Thank the Lord that some has fallen in good soil, and that you and I have the great privilege of watering and feeding it. Remember always that 'it is God who gives the growth' (1 Cor 3:7).

11

Marrying a Clergyman

'Oh, Cynthia, I've got the jitters! I love Paul very much, and I'm sure it's right for us to marry, but I just can't think of myself as the minister's wife!' Chris, like many brides-to-be, was suffering from an acute attack of pre-wedding nerves. She had known Paul ever since he had come, fresh from college, to be the assistant minister in her home church some three years previously. It was not until he had moved into another situation six months ago that their romance had blossomed, and now with a week to go to the wedding, she was panicking at the thought of all that she might be letting herself in for.

Unfortunately Chris had acquired a very wrong view of 'the minister's wife'. The only one that she had really known was in fact a very capable lady, who could organize an annual bunfight or lead the church Bible study with equal ease. Around her, in Chris's mind, had grown a bright aura which set her very much apart from other mortal beings. Now she, Chris, had got to match up to this paragon, and it seemed impossible!

If you have stayed with me through the previous chapters, I'm sure you will have realized something of what is involved in the life of a clergy wife. Now, for the sake of people like Chris about to embark on a lifetime of ministry in this particular way, I want to enumerate some of the practical dos and don'ts:

1. Do be yourself. You are not 'Superspiritualwoman', and generally not expected to be. Don't try to model yourself on another minister's wife. It never works. Underneath you are you, and before long that real you will emerge anyway.

   Remember that the Lord, who put you in this position, has also equipped you to serve him. Probably you have many God-inspired gifts which you will spend your lifetime in developing and using, just like all Christians. Don't expect them all to surface immediately your husband accepts the pastoral charge of a local church. Be natural, and let your personal involvement with church life grow gently.

2. Don't neglect your own devotional life. It is your lifeline. Because you are where you are in the spiritual battle-line, the attacks will be forceful, so you must be protected, and in a position to build up your defences. Often there are early morning calls, your days will be busy, and entertaining, counselling and such like sometimes stretches late into the night, so it is not always easy to fit in a time alone with the Lord each day, but do it, nonetheless. It is essential.

3. Pray for your husband daily. You will no doubt pray with him for every aspect of your ministry together, but he also needs your supportive prayer. As you know him better than most people, you will also know in what areas of his life he needs special prayer, but do especially pray that God will keep him true to the Bible and its teaching.

   The head-on spiritual attack does not always come by way of illness or accident. Far more frequently it is in a subtle, insidious thought or idea which is not quite true to the overall teaching of Scripture. Your husband needs your prayers, that his understanding of the Bible will be kept pure and unadulterated.

4. Do encourage your better half in his ministry. Some congregations are quick to criticize when they discover a flaw, but painfully slow in offering a word of appreciation. In any case, there will be times when he will feel like throwing it all in, and joining the nine to five brigade again. That is when he especially needs your support and love. The people in the pew won't understand this, so it is up to you.

5. Make sure that you have a day off together each week. This will mean actually leaving the house, I'm afraid, away from the telephone, callers and studybooks. Tedious perhaps in the winter months, but essential if you are really to relax. If you do stay home, the phone invariably rings incessantly, and even if it doesn't, you are half expecting it to do so, and that does not constitute a relaxed, feet-up, let-your-hair-down sort of day.

One minister I know has a caravan a few miles away from home, on a friend's farm. He and his wife frequently retire there on a sunny day off, armed with Agatha Christie and an oil-painting kit, returning refreshed in the early evening.

Another couple use their free days to visit friends from a wide radius, or make shopping expeditions to nearby towns.

A sporting young curate and his wife have a tennis date every Wednesday morning, followed by a snack lunch in a favourite restaurant, and a riverside walk in the afternoon.

The message really is: whatever is your fun thing, get out and do it. You both need a regular break if you are to give your best to the people the Lord has given into your spiritual care.

6. There may be times when members of the congregation will try to use you as a vehicle, whereby they can express

their criticisms of the minister or the church. Always be loyal to your husband. Never take sides. Ask the Lord for tact and discernment in these matters.

7. Remember that whatever you may say about another Christian in front of your children will condition their thinking concerning that person. Therefore, where the members of your congregation are concerned, be careful what you discuss at the meal table or wherever you are together as a family.

8. Be wise in the general use of your home. If there is a constant state of 'open-house', or if too many meetings are held there, your children could feel themselves to be in the way.

   'You're not pushing us out of the lounge again, are you?' exploded my young son one evening, as I re-organized the furniture for a house-group Bible study.

   Make sure that you know where your priorities lie.

9. Accept your children as a gift from the Lord. Never regard them as a hindrance to your work. Invest a lot of time, thought and energy in them while they are young. In years to come it will pay dividends. Your contribution to the 'church family' will be more valuable if you are a Christian mum who has discharged her responsibility well.

10. Recognize that others within your church fellowship will have gifts which differ from your own. Respect those gifts; help to develop them if possible; never covet them for yourself. Discover your own special talents, and use them.

11. Don't have 'special friends' within the church. Endeavour to treat everybody in the same way. Some people you will find particularly difficult to get on with. Ask the Lord to give you his love for them especially.

12. Remember that you can only please some of the people some of the time. There are times when you or your husband will have to take a leading decision which

affects others within the church. Not everyone will agree with you, but provided you have come to that decision prayerfully, in the best interests of the congregation, they will mostly respect your decisiveness.

13. Be prepared for disappointments. People will sometimes let you down. Some who showed great promise as committed Christians will lose interest and be caught away by the lure of 'the world'. Some who volunteer to take responsibility within the local fellowship will run out of steam and become unreliable.

14. Be willing to accept other people's kindness. Sometimes it is difficult to be on the receiving end, especially when we spend much of our lives giving out. Perhaps it is a kind of perverted independence.

'Why didn't you ask me to help you?' said my friend, after I had struggled through a particular problem alone.

'I didn't want to put you to any trouble,' I replied.

'So now you've deprived me of the joy of helping you,' she said. And she was right.

Jesus said, 'It is more blessed to give than to receive.' Perhaps we could let some of that blessedness rub off on some of our friends a little more often, as we allow them to give of themselves to us.

15. Sometimes you will fail in your ministry. When you know this, don't let the Enemy score a complete victory by keeping you down. Remind yourself of chapter 18 in Jeremiah's prophecy, where the Lord gave to him a lovely illustration. Jeremiah watched a potter making a vessel which, as it grew on his trundling wheel, did not turn out as he had intended. It was supposed to be a beautiful vessel, displaying the delicate touch of its creator, but it was out of shape, bent in the wrong places! It should have been a reliable utensil, able to stand up to the knocks of life, but this one never would.

The thing that really interests me is that the mis-shapen pot was not marked 'reject', or sold at half price. It was remade 'as it seemed good to the potter to do' (Jer 18:4).

Is not that just what our wonderful Creator, Father God does for us when we come humbly to him for forgiveness? He refashions us as it seems good to the Master Potter to do. Once again we become, not just clay in his hand, but a 'chosen vessel' (Acts 9:15 Authorized Version) through whom the Lord himself can reveal his glory to those in our care.

You might sometimes be down, but there is no need to be down and out!

16. Beware of putting your roots down too deeply in any one place. It will hurt a lot more when the time comes to pull up and transplant! Occasionally one hears of ministers staying in one church for twenty or thirty years, but that is rare. Probably the average is about ten, but it is often much less, so we need to be prepared to move on while, at the same time, giving all we have got to the present situation.

17. If possible, and try to make it so, acquire a hobby or interest outside of your church commitment. Dress-making, a flower club, an evening class, a sport that will help to keep you healthy as well as absorb your mind—whatever you find stimulating and refreshing, let it serve to refresh your whole person. Even Christian work can become a drudge!

18. Expect to be on twenty-four hour call, but don't feel guilty about not working all the time. Nobody really expects you to, and the Lord did not plan it that way. It is easy to feel 'caught out' by a visiting parishioner if you happen to have your feet up when they call. Don't feel ashamed of such lethargy! And don't make excuses for yourself. It is your right to relax now and then, and it is absolutely necessary if you are to be effective in

your work.

19. If possible, make friends with another clergy couple, who live far enough away not to be on intimate terms with any of your parishioners. All four of you will find it helpful to 'talk shop' occasionally. Often another mind with a sympathetic understanding of your kind of situation will throw light on a particular problem which you might have.

Apart from this, it is good to relax with others of like mind and common interests.

20. Don't think of your local fellowship as 'your work'. It is the Lord's work. You are only managing it for him, under his sole direction. Any blessing that results from your labours is on his initiative. It all revolves around him.

It was right for Chris to be a little apprehensive. She realized that she was not only about to take solemn vows regarding her commitment to marriage, but also that this particular marriage would put her into a position where certain demands and expectations would be made of her. She really felt very inadequate, and her natural shyness made her shrink from all that she thought would be expected of her.

Three years later, when I was preparing to write this book, I contacted Chris, asking her to give me her impressions of what it's all about. Particularly, I thought, she might help with some of the negative sides of our situation, the problems we have to face with adapting to being in the limelight of church life, the pressures of keeping up with all that it is assumed we can do, the difficulties of having to share our husbands with many other people.

Instead she wrote a glowing letter, listing thirteen privileges which she had found during those three years of marriage, and not one single moan! Many of these joys have been sprinkled through the preceding chapters.

Perhaps it is largely summed up in her appraisal of those first days together in the ministry:

'I found that, unexpectedly, I had been so prayed about, so talked about, and so wanted, that the warmth of welcome was quite overwhelming! Everyone knows who I am, so I am always acknowledged when walking into my home church. I feel as though I count in the community.'

Head cook and bottle-washer, leader of the Women's Own, putter-up of many guests, her husband's personal secretary, sitter on various committees, a trouble shooter at home and in church life too, a shoulder to cry on whenever needed, a listening ear to many troubles. A clergyman's wife has a varied life. Never can it be labelled 'boring'; sometimes it is positively exhilarating!

So you are going to marry a clergyman too? Don't unless you know it is God's will for you both. If it is and you do, there is great joy ahead.

When the honeymoon is over, and the hard graft starts; when the enemy attacks come on strong; when responsibility weighs heavily on your shoulders; you might well wonder why you ever chose this particular path through life! But when you take on the role of spiritual midwife and watch a toddler group mum become a brand new believer; when you see your Bible class girls growing up to build happy Christian homes; when you witness a flood of peace washing over a worried brow as you pray with a hurting soul—you'll know that you are in the right place. You will say, as I have said: 'I married the minister, and I'm glad I did.'

Leading Ladies

Women of the Bible speak to leaders' wives today

by Wendy Virgo

Adam—Moses—David—Samson—Job

—each had a wife who either supported his life and ministry, or contributed to its downfall. Queen Esther had her own unique role. What can we learn from these and other leading ladies of the past?

Wendy Virgo skilfully retells and examines the biblical stories, to show leaders' wives today how they can fulfil their roles in a high-pressure world. Whether you are married to an itinerant preacher or a youth-group leader, you will find principles to help develop a ministry that both supports and complements that of your husband.

> *Wendy has sought to display the biblical picture of a woman not crushed into mindless submission but released into fulfilling ministry through honest observance of the biblical safeguards.*
> Terry Virgo

Wendy Virgo is respected for her ministry to leaders' wives in many churches. She is married to well-known church leader Terry Virgo, and they have five children.

Kingsway Publications

Queen take your throne
How to be a woman of authority

by Eileen Wallis

We are living in a time of spiritual awakening. As the church comes alive, God's men are taking their rightful place of leadership.

Can a woman also exercise authority?

From the biblical story of Esther, Eileen Wallis shows that every Christian woman is indeed called to a position of authority. In straightforward, practical terms she shows what that means for both single and married women, as they follow their Lord's commission to reign in life in a kingdom of righteousness and peace.

k
Kingsway Publications

Growing Together

by Clive & Ruth Calver

Meet Clive, the rough-and-ready radical.
He's going to marry Ruth, the Bible college
principal's daughter...

With warmth and refreshing honesty, Clive and
Ruth Calver draw from their own experience
valuable principles to guide Christians through the
ups and downs of married life. Often humorous,
always instructive, they take us through the heady
days of courtship, on to a mature, Christ-centred
marriage, not flinching for a moment from
revealing the pitfalls along the way.

Here too we see how a Christian family can be a
practical source of help to the unmarried, and a
beacon of stability in a society that has gone adrift.
All those contemplating marriage—as well as those
who like Clive and Ruth look back over several
years of married life—will find here food for
thought and ideas for action.

Clive Calver is General Secretary of the Evangelical Alliance.
He and Ruth have been married for fourteen years, and have
two sons and two daughters.

Kingsway Publications

My Family, My Church

by Rob & Marion White

A family is a place of togetherness, where people of all ages can be themselves and minister to each other.

And so is a church.

Yet for many parents the pleasures and duties of family life conflict with those of church life. Meanwhile many church leaders find that families—and especially children—fit uncomfortably into the local church fellowship.

Rob and Marion White are convinced that this tension is unnecessary. Drawing on their own experience of both church leadership and parenthood, they provide here *encouragement* to parents in distress and *a radical challenge* to the church to review its attitude to children as members of Christ's body.

Rob White is National Director of British Youth for Christ. Marion is a trained infant teacher. The front cover shows them with their three children, Jo, Debbie and Naomi.

K

Kingsway Publications